"*Dear Future Me* lets us eavesdrop on the silly, serious, hilarious and heartbreaking conversations that ordinary people have with the extraordinary people they hope—or fear—they will someday become, providing a fascinating view of the human mind on its one-way trip through time."

—Daniel Gilbert, professor of psychology, Harvard University; best-selling author of *Stumbling on Happiness*

"Most of the great philosophers have struggled to define this elusive thing called Self. Plato, Descartes, Locke, Hume—they all gave slightly different answers to the same haunting question: Who am I? FutureMe.org freshens this age-old question by reframing it in e-mail-ese, the telegraphic code of our daily lives, which creates a sharper sense of immediacy than the prosaic letter. Forced to address ourselves through the language and lens of a new technology, one that stretches and shortens our notion of time, we can't help but ask: Is this me at 42 the same me I will be at 62? Am I just one me in the midst of a single unified narrative, or a series of mes connected by one strand of memories, one starting point, one name?"

—J.R. Moehringer, Pulitzer Prize–winning correspondent, *L.A. Times*; best-selling author of *The Tender Bar: A Memoir*

"The relationship between Present Me and Future Me is too often a parental one: I'm forever making decisions on behalf of Future Me, who I treat like an incompetent man-child—leaving to-do lists where he'll find them, signing his name to employment contracts and bank loans, educating him, tattooing him, and fattening him up. But must things go on this way forever? Shouldn't the Mes have a more evolved relationship? Absolutely, insist the contributors to *Dear Future Me*, who may sometimes lecture their self-to-come, but who more often treat that special someone as a confidant, comrade, accomplice, collaborator, maybe even a pal. 'I know you'll badmouth me sometimes, and I'm sure I deserve it,' one e-mailer writes. 'But I'm pulling for you.' Spoken like a true friend."

—Joshua Glenn, columnist, Ideas section of *The Boston Globe*; editor of *Taking Things Seriously*

"Dear Future Me spills over with all of life's pain, wonder, and mystery. These peeks inside the heads and hearts of strangers are magical; we can't help but recognize ourselves. This book is funny, profound, and endlessly absorbing—I could not put it down!"

—Davy Rothbart, founder and editor of *FOUND* magazine; contributor, *This American Life*

Dear Future Me

HOW
BOOKS

Cincinnati, Ohio
www.howdesign.com

Dear Future Me

Me ✉

hopes, fears, secrets, resolutions

edited by MATT SLY & JAY PATRIKIOS,
creators of FutureMe.org

3 1257 01718 5918

For more fine books from F+W Publications, visit www.fwbookstore.com.

11 10 09 08 07   5 4 3 2 1

Distributed in Canada by Fraser Direct, 100 Armstrong Avenue, Georgetown, Ontario, Canada L7G 5S4, Tel: (905) 877-4411. Distributed in the U.K. and Europe by David & Charles, Brunel House, Newton Abbot, Devon, TQ12 4PU, England, Tel: (+44) 1626 323200, Fax: (+44) 1626 323319, E-mail: postmaster@davidandcharles.co.uk. Distributed in Australia by Capricorn Link, P.O. Box 704, Windsor, NSW 2756 Australia, Tel: (02) 4577-3555.

Library of Congress Cataloging-in-Publication Data

Dear future me : hopes, fears, secrets, resolutions / edited by Matt Sly and Jay Patrikios.
      p. cm.
   ISBN 978-1-58180-977-0 (pbk. : alk. paper)
   1. Expectation (Psychology) 2. Self-fulfilling prophecy. 3. Introspection.
   4. Electronic mail messages. I. Sly, Matt. II. Patrikios, Jay.
   BF323.E8D43 2007
   155.2'5--dc22   2007019356

Edited by Amy Schell
Designed by Grace Ring
Production coordinated by Greg Nock

F•W PUBLICATIONS, INC.

DEDICATION

To Anna and Mia. And to the future, for always being there.

ACKNOWLEDGMENTS

Jay and Matt would like to thank our families; our friends (especially the Friday night Trivial Pursuit kids—and even Shefali, who thought that our idea was lame); the people at F+W Publications for making this book look so damn good, with a special thanks to our very fantastic editor, Amy Schell; the hundreds of bloggers who helped spread the word about FutureMe.org; and everyone who contributed an e-mail—public (but anonymous) or private—to FutureMe.org. Keep 'em coming.

Introduction

FutureMe.org began—like many small ideas that eventually become less small—with a conversation over a Friday night round of burritos and a game of three-on-three Trivial Pursuit.

While we struggled to recall the dates of the Ottoman Empire and the names of 1980s television stars, we started talking about just how inaccurate memories are. Then someone (probably Matt) mentioned those letters some of us had to write on the first day of freshman year that were collected by guidance counselors and distributed back to us four years later on graduation day. Which led us to wonder why only high school kids should get to write letters to their future selves. And might a website be able to serve as a *life-long* guidance counselor—dutifully delivering letters to our future selves?

We determined that building such a site would provide an ample opportunity to showcase Matt's mad database skills and Jay's then-crush on teeny-tiny fonts. So over the next month or so, in an hour of free time here, and a moment of procrastination there, we built FutureMe.org.

The idea is simple: Write a letter to yourself, choose whether you want it to be public or private, and then we send it to you at some point in the future—you pick the date. Public letters are displayed on the site for all to read. Private ones are kept private, obviously, and not even read by us.

We told a few friends and figured that was that. Apparently, those friends told other friends, who must have told other friends, because we started getting a lot of "hits" (as we say in the biz). And then we were on Webmonkey. And then we were selected as a Yahoo! Pick of the Day.

But the fun was just beginning. We ended up being featured in the largest museum of digital art in the world, which is in Austria. Of course. Matt did a radio interview with a station in Ireland while driving through Canada. Jay got a 6 A.M. phone call from some Scottish lawyer. (Have you ever tried to decipher Scottish at 6 A.M.? It's very difficult.) We got weird e-mails from people who had done strange things with FutureMe.org, like this guy who wanted to retrieve a letter in which he put his Hotmail password that wasn't going to be delivered until 2011. (Bad idea!)

In December 2005, The Associated Press released a little story about FutureMe.org that was picked up all over the world by hundreds of publications. Our poor little web hosting company was deluged. We still feel kind of bad about that. And we did some interviews on outlets like National Public Radio, CNN and Radio Free Chico.

It was about this time that the nice folks over at F+W Publications approached us about doing a compilation of FutureMe letters. Hence this book.

As of this printing, there are nearly 400,000 letters written to future selves, a fraction of which were designated public and are on the site for your perusal. We read that (much-larger-than-you-would-think) fraction and whittled it down to 230 letters for inclusion in the book.

Some of the e-mails made us laugh out loud, several inspired prolonged existential contemplation, and a few had us putting our hands up to our faces, peeking through our fingers and hoping that the people who wrote them would turn out okay (be okay, please be okay). We fully expect that this collection will rouse similar reactions in you, brave reader.

The future is indeed a curiosity—our past selves of that night in San Francisco certainly did not anticipate that their future selves would publish a book based on their silly idea. Our journey to the present has been entertaining, bizarre, rewarding and almost entirely unpredictable. And you know what? Hooray for an unpredictable future.

Take care,
Matt and Jay

EDITORS' NOTE

For the most part, we have left the letters in the form in which they were written, although some letters have been edited for length. Spelling, grammar and punctuation errors (or perhaps "reinterpretations") remain throughout the book. After much deliberation, we decided that taking this approach would more accurately preserve the tone and context of the letters and—perhaps more important—the nature of e-mail as a medium. This book is meant to document how we engage with both our future selves and with technology. In many cases, this interaction is as unpolished as it is provocative.

Statistics

A sample of statistics from FutureMe.org: a pretty much wholly unscientific investigation of how people interact with the future.

Total number of letters written, as of May 1, 2007:

396,610

Letters that are public: 7%

How far into the future the letters are sent:

1 year (44%)   20 years (1%)

5 years (5%)   30 years (2%)

10 years (3%)

Most popular send day:
December 19

11,133 letters, 2.8% of the total number of letters

(Note: December 19, 2005, is the day that The Associated Press released a story featuring FutureMe.org, and the default send date is one year.)

Second most popular send day:
January 1

10,721 letters, 2.7% of the total number of letters

Some popular terms that appear in letters:

love (19.3%)

job (6.8%)

family (4.1%)

money (3.0%)

fat (2.9%)

health (2.4%)

sex (2.0%)

parents (1.9%)

weight (1.7%)

children (1.2%)

depressed (0.7%)

Jesus (0.5%)

exercise (0.4%)

George Bush (0.3%)

bald (0.3%)

Most letters written to a single e-mail address:

1074

(since December 19, 2005—that's more than one per day)

The Letters

Dear FutureMe,

It's nice to know you exist. I can't wait for you to happen!!! You've been an odd thing to look forward to. I don't want to complain about what you've done before, and how you threw those unpleasant surprises at me and all that, but if I had to choose you to be my future again, I totally would. Thanks for everything. But most of all, thanks for being so enigmatic and unknown. I love being a little scared of you…And I love not knowing. Ah well, I guess you and I have less talking to do and more living. So see you soon! Bye! Oops! There you are. Hehehe…

WRITTEN: December 01, 2005
SENT: December 01, 2006

Dear FutureMe,

I hope I am still with David, because I am going to get his name tattooed today. So if I'm not, I'll probably be laughing when I read this.

WRITTEN: February 18, 2006
SENT: April 01, 2007

407 days

Dear FutureMe,

He is alive today, but will be gone now that you're reading this. Remember that nothing ever disappears, only changes form. He loves you today. Even with the pain of the cancer throughout his entire body, he is kind. No one has ever loved you so completely and without condition! He said he hopes someday someone else will love you as well as he has, remember? Remember that love at this moment and be grateful for the experiences you were able to share. Remember all he has taught and given you. Use it well in his memory and know that he will always love you this way. You've come far, but have farther to go yet.

WRITTEN: January 17, 2006
SENT: January 01, 2007

Dear FutureMe,

Don't ask Brandon out. Ever!

WRITTEN: December 20, 2005
SENT: December 20, 2006

Dear FutureMe,

I decided this morning to live like FutureMe. I decided if I did that I would learn to truly accept myself in the present. It means I can do exactly what I want to do with no more excuses. No more "I can't do that because I'm too fat," "too poor," "not good enough," etc., etc. FutureMe doesn't have any of those problems. If I live like FutureMe, I will become FutureMe. At least that's the theory.

And then I just did a search for "Future Me" on the net just to see what came up and found this site. Cool idea.

So FutureMe, when you receive this I hope you're in a better place than I am right now. Hope you're over that health problem, hope you're getting up and singing your heart out, hope you've finished that novel, hope you're in loads less debt. I hope you're helping people. And I hope you're not FutureMe any more, but PresentMe. Does that make sense?

> **"I decided this morning to live like FutureMe. I decided if I did that I would learn to truly accept myself in the present."**

I hope you can look back when you receive this (how cool would it be if you forgot you wrote it and it was a total surprise!) and feel bloody great that you moved on from this point.

Love,
PresentMe

WRITTEN: June 04, 2005
SENT: June 06, 2006

Dear FutureMe,

Happy 40th birthday. Are you at the age when you won't reveal your age? Because if you are, your 14 year old self is telling you that that is silly.

You're married, I suppose? To whom? Whoever he is, he's really lucky. :)

I guess you have kids as well. Be fair to them. Try and put yourself in my mind. Don't do anything they wouldn't want. Although that probably isn't the best advice. *imagines what life would be like if MY parents did that*

Anyway, I hope you have a wonderful birthday, and I hope you've put the last 25 years to good use.

Love,
PastMe

WRITTEN: February 20, 2006
SENDING: November 06, 2031

The brightest moments between birth and death:

1974, Summer, which for some reason stays in my mind as one of the best summers from my childhood, the holidays seemed to last forever, the sky was bluer than I can remember it being since, all was well with the world…

- - - - - - - - - -

1977, Teenage life: The Jam, Deep Purple, Bowie, girls, etc…

- - - - - - - - - -

1998, between 19th and 27th Dec: Rose Street… the one and only time where I had a perfect little box to live in, everything ordered and in it's place with plenty money in the bank. New movies (which I knew would be great) yet to watch, new music from my favorite bands yet to hear, amazingly cool games that I had only begun playing and several books from my favorite authors yet to read.

Needless to say, the very second I realised that I had attained this comfortable state I set about getting rid of it all.

- - - - - - - - - -

Aegean, night, fishing boats: I remember sitting on the shore of Naxos Island, a warm night and a full belly, out at sea I watched the distant soundless lights of fishing boats moving to and fro...

- - - - - - - - - -

Paris, a night of wild sex with two beautiful women. Nuff said...

- - - - - - - - - -

Arriving at Finisterra having walked there from Le Puy... I should have turned left and gone to Portugal, not right and returned to Scotland... I have never felt so well, in both mind and body, my life was never filled with so much potential...

- - - - - - - - - -

Sleeping beside my camp fire in the Namibian bush.

WRITTEN: December 31, 2005
SENT: December 31, 2006

hey FutureMe,

just letting you know that I'm enjoying my youthful vigor, my full head of hair and my flat belly... before I turn into you.

WRITTEN: January 21, 2003
SENDING: January 01, 2010

11

Dear FutureMe:

Last night you were so bored you cut your hair. You gave yourself bangs that you swore at one time you would never wear again and now every time mum looks at you, she says, "You look so cute!"

Try not to do this again.

WRITTEN: January 08, 2006
SENDING: May 22, 2009

Dear FutureMe,

happy 21st birthday. if you have a single drop of alcohol you will hate yourself forever. remember dad. remember his drinking. how it made you feel. the things he said. the things he did. don't EVER be him.

remember promising yourself you'd never a touch a drop? you'd never be like him? you'd never hurt anyone the way that he hurt you? how messed up he's made you?

follow through.
don't drink.

don't drink.

don't drink.

don't you dare drink.

hopeful,

teenage you

WRITTEN: March 16, 2006

SENDING: May 09, 2009

Dear FutureMe,

At the time of this writing:

1. You'd been married 9 yrs & 4 months to the day (but who's counting?)!

2. Your husband has 34 months left til retirement as a Navy Air Traffic Controller.

3. You have 3 children—V. (5), R. (3) and C. (23 months) AND you're trying for #4! (Hope that wish came true!)

4. Your dream home is a log cabin of 2000+ sq. ft. in the mountains somewhere.

5. Your dream "job" is to own and rent out log cabin suites in the mountains.

6. You'd like at least 1 more girl, but would be happy with 3 more kids (2 girls and a boy)!

7. Your mom is still alive & ticking (barely) in upstate NY freezing her butt off!

8. You have 2 brothers living still in Orlando.

9. You have 11 nieces and nephews, 2 great-nieces & a great-nephew.

10. You weigh only 117.5 lbs … still and are 5 ft. 2.5 in.

11. You're in debt $72,534.68 including those stupid student loans
    that started out at $13,000 and are $33,000 to date because of com-
    pounding interest!

12. You've always wanted to: go to Hawaii, go on a cruise to Alaska, take a
    hot air balloon ride, take ballroom dance lessons, finish scrapbooking,
    record a CD of yourself singing, have a nice tan & a firm tummy …

It's been 3 years since you wrote this and now you're almost 35 so STOP
MAKING LISTS & GET GOING!!!!!!!

Love You!

WRITTEN: January 07, 2006
SENDING: January 07, 2009

Dear FutureMe,

I would like to ask a lot later version of you but I don't know how long
this e-mail is going to last. What the hell are you doing right now? Are
you back with N. or are you hating yourself because you let her slip
away? Are you still going into the music business or have you decided it
was best to do something more lucrative. I wish you could come visit me,
take me by the hand, and tell me that everything is all right. I'm pretty
much at rock bottom right now. I lost my job, I lost the love of my life,
and I have this pain in my back that won't seem to go away. I've hit bottom enough that I'm writing to my future self on this stupid website. You
can't get much worse than that. I read some other people's entries and

they made me cry. I realize that I am not the only one suffering in the world. I hope things are better now. It is your birthday. Are you doing anything exciting? You better be.

> **"I wish you could come visit me, take me by the hand, and tell me that everything is all right."**

I really don't love myself right now. I mean, how could I? I'm left with nothing. Hopefully this finds you doing much better than I am. Call your friends. I'm sure they miss you. Call N., wherever she may be.

WRITTEN: August 02, 2006
SENT: August 31, 2007

Dear FutureMe,

If you are still a virgin by this date, give up on waiting for love and go fuck for Christ's sake. Make sure the guy has no obvious ills, make sure he wears a condom, and just fuck. Feel it.

You've waited long enough, and you shouldn't feel guilty or dirty for wanting to. You don't really believe in God, but since you've been a good person all your life and it hasn't done shit to allow you to meet Mr. Right, go find someone to fuck. Now. Do it. Craigslist, at a bar, a friend, whatever. Just have your first fuck and enjoy the remainder of your twenties.

WRITTEN: December 19, 2005
SENT: December 19, 2006

Hey,

I've been putting off writing this letter for a week or so. In part, because I'm not sure what to type. Everything seems so mundane to say to one's future self. Although I'm sure that it's the mundane that is the most important in life.

Tomorrow, we turn 35. I didn't send this to us when we were 30 because I figure things will be much the same at that time. But 35 seems so far off. Does 24 seem more than a decade ago?

So far, there are only a few things I can count that I've done for more than a decade: my friendship with K., JBS, performing, using the word 'hella', living in the Northwest (well, for the most part).

> "Do I still have issues with living in the moment? Do I believe in Heaven? Am I still self-centered?"

What things that I do in 2006 am I doing in 2016? Am I living in Seattle? Am I living with C.? Is Dad alive? Am I performing? Do I still have issues with living in the moment? Do I believe in Heaven? Am I still self-centered?

I hope we've learned how to knit more than just one stitch. I hope we can do consistent triple turns on both legs. I hope we've hiked to the top of Mt. Rainier. I hope we've figured out what tattoo I should get. I hope we haven't broken any more bones, or spent a lot of time in the hospital.

In 2006, you are pretty friggin happy. You felt well rested (for the most part). You could lose five pounds, but have finally decided that feeling good is more important than looking good. You drink a shit load of diet coke. You spend a lot of time watching Netflix, walking around Seattle, going to dance class. You feel like things are just going to get better, more exciting, more fulfilling.

Things are good right now. I think I'm honestly happier than almost everyone I encounter. I hope that I am still this positive.

WRITTEN: January 29, 2006
SENDING: June 22, 2016

So FutureMe, did you quit your job and move to New York to go back to college? If so, you are probably hungry and poor. So go look in your dictionary next to the word "hungry." You'll find a $5 stashed there. Go buy a happy meal at McDonalds and stop complaining about having no money.

WRITTEN: September 10, 2003
SENT: September 09, 2004

365 days

Dear FutureMe,

You seem to be doing quite well at present. Quite well is a relative term. I mean, you're not really doing anything important or significant, or anything that you really seem to give a crap about, but you're not dead. Nor are you in an abusive relationship, or addicted to cocaine.

The worst things in your life right now are your immeasurable debt to Visa, and you appear to be in the beginning stages of alcoholism. Don't say you didn't see it coming, because I'm calling it right now. Don't be too proud to go to AA. I'm pretty sure AA's can still drink a beer every now and then. (Actually, FutureMe, PastMe is getting kind of impatient, as you are currently putting off going to the bar RIGHT NOW to write this frickin' email.)

As well a drinker, you're currently a gung-ho smoker. Your cigarette of choice is the Lucky Strike brand, mostly because of their fun little inserts, encouraging smokers to keep on keeping on. You seem to have become quite the connoisseur, as you won't 'bum' cigarettes off anyone smoking Marlboros or most things Camel, or anything menthol. If it's not a Lucky, it's not worth smoking. Okay, that's not true, because you'll smoke either Dave's brand (you like the fact that a guy named a cigarette after himself), or American Spirits (the hipsters back in Moscow used to smoke them, and even though you don't really enjoy American Spirits, you know you look pretty cool carrying them).

Enough about you, though, FutureMe, this is all old news from you, and you have a very well documented diary to look back on the years. Let's divulge some of my expectations for you.

First, you expect yourself to be making much more money than you are right now. You're not expecting an actual salary, but you're making $10.81/hour right now, and you'd like to see something around the $18–$20 range.

You're not calling yourself a failure if you're not at this point, this is just what you're currently expecting.

Second, you should still be a smoker. If you're not, you should have taken the precaution of hiding an emergency pack for you somewhere you're sure to be in three years. Swear to god, you're putting a pack of Lucky Strikes in a metal box and burying it in your mother's back yard. If you're not a smoker, please go uncover the box and smoke them right now. Go ahead, I'll wait. You'll thank yourself for this. Hey, also as a side note, just less than two weeks ago, Washington State passed a new law that you can't smoke inside any type of business, bar, disco tech and night club included. You are very, very offended at this law, although you didn't vote against or for it (at all, you know? You've got something unidentifiable against the idea of voting, and you're not even registered) so you're keeping your mouth shut.

Next, you want to have been in a serious relationship by this time. It's fine if you're single right now, you don't mind, but you're hoping you've had that experience under your belt. At present, you've only got C. in your past, and we really need his relevance to falter. You don't seem to have any prospects in your sights right now. I mean, there's a gentleman here and there that strikes your fancy, but you seem to find some reason not to bother. You're not sure if your expectations are too high, or your self esteem is too low, but you seem to be really good at making excuses. The latest prospect is a (younger!) man named J., and you've managed to put off calling him for close to three weeks, and the excuse you're using is that, last time you spoke, he was gearing up to start a new job in the pest control industry. Think on that one for a while. Your 'Other Me' seems to find it pretty valid, based on your current standings for animal rights.

FutureMe, you're babbling right now, and you're really impatient because if you want to go to the bar and be home by 1:00a (you wake up at 6:30 am, FYI), you're cutting it really freaking close. This displeases you. Future L., you will receive a follow up email within the next several days. Promises!

FutureMe, whatever is going on in your life right now, you just hope you've reached some sort of contentment. This nothingness you're putting yourself through is a real drag. At least, get us a hobby.

I LOVE YOU!! You're spectacular! AND BEAUTIFUL!!

WRITTEN: December 20, 2005

SENDING: November 19, 2008

Dear FutureMe,

You better had quit that fucking drinking during the day i dont care if u dont get drunk im sick of this goddamn crutch that you have every body has pain lose the rest of your weight damn it!!!!!!!!!!!!! Did u lose 50 60 lbs for nothing finish the last 50 get beautiful on the outside cause u sure as hell are on the inside stop being scared its ok we can do this together fuck a man!!!!!!!!!!!!! You are hot and u know it so why do u act like you need to be so so fucking lame. You have so so so much going for you you are better than this!!! Quit it now and you better have stopped taking pills (i dont know how to stop any of this) get in church ask for help (but im scared of telling anyone i dont want them to know im a failure) your not a failure get up and off it i dont want to hear no more excuse like i dont do it every day or i havent done it today i bet u did it yesterday or will tomorrow

And u smoke pot everyday dont u even if u skipped today i dont care

Sssssssttttttoooooopppppppp iiiiiiiiiiiiiiiiiiiittttttttt

Its aging you and destroying your organs

Are you still bulimic????????

Damn it stop or u wont see your kids grow up you will be dead!!!!!!!

WRITTEN: January 12, 2006
SENT: March 03, 2006

Dear FutureMe,

I am extremely confused! One day I am hopeful about the future, and the next, totally hopeless. I hope that by this time the people of America will have gotten rid of the horribly evil administration and senate and house politicians that have absolutely no concern for the people of the US and the world. Bush has a 35 to 40 percent approval rating and 2065 have died in Iraq because of his lies. A covert CIA operative and her entire career protecting us from WMD's has been exposed and no one has paid any price for it. Libby has just been indicted. Cooperations now run America through their evil aides Bush, Cheney, Rumsfield, Rice, Wolfowitz, & etc. Hopefully when I receive this things will have changed for the better.

I do love my new BIGGER apartment though. :-)

WRITTEN: November 12, 2005
SENT: November 12, 2006

> **"One day I am hopeful about the future, and the next, totally hopeless."**

Dear FutureMe,

sometimes you think that you have no future in creative writing and really should adopt something more practical, more fitting of your skills.

which is to walk around going LA LA LA LA

which is what a creative writing MFA is starting to sound like.

so far you're biggest writing achievement is making out with a somewhat famous professor.

you're afraid you're going to be a loser by the time you graduate.

now that you have, please prove you/me wrong.

(I know there will come a time when that you/me thing will no longer amuse you/me, but right now, me thinks you wont)

WRITTEN: February 21, 2006
SENT: May 20, 2007

Dear FutureJ.,

I will be receiving this email on what would have been our eighth wedding anniversary. Today is December 28, 2005. I am writing this because I have had an epiphany about my own understanding of what has happened between us and what I need to remember and hang on to and never long to return to this marriage.

Tonight as I was watching TV, it suddenly occurred to me that I should no longer be asking how could you, F., hate me or be so selfish that you could do these things to me, to us, to our family. Rather I must continually ask myself how could I hate MYSELF enough to want this relationship knowing your capacity for deceit, selfishness, callousness and betrayal.

This is an important switch in my thinking, and as I continued with this line of thinking, again bits and pieces of the absolute horror and selfishness of your acts opened to me. In my mind seeing you lie in our bed holding another woman and smiling and laughing with her when our wedding pictures were on the wall only five feet away. How you kissed her and entered her body in the bed our son was conceived in and in the same bed that you lay beside me and told me you loved me with all your heart.

> **"I have to remember these things and carry them with me, brandishing these scars on my heart as symbols of the possibility for rebirth, for growth, for strength."**

No amount of confusion, desperateness or longing justifies the level of betrayal you have meted out on me. My marriage, my home, my heart, the only places I ever felt safe and loved, were violated and disrespected out of nothing more than sheer selfishness and immaturity. I have to think of your hands on my stomach that carried our son and remember how your face smiled and your voice said you loved me while your heart betrayed me and wrote love letters to a simple whore. I have to remember these things and carry them with me, brandishing these scars on my heart as symbols of the possibility and the hope, the need for rebirth, for growth, for STRENGTH.

I don't hate myself for loving you, I will love you until I die—nothing will ever change that. We shared our life, dreams, families, years and we will always share a beautiful son. I will hate myself for accepting a marriage in which I was betrayed, and used. Another thing I realized is that, for you, a large part of your attraction to me originally was the glow in my eyes that reflected back to you that someone valued you and saw you as perfect—when you yourself had no love for yourself. You have confidence in your abilities and drive, but I don't believe you have ever loved yourself, and as a result you have never loved anyone else as a partner, a lover, a friend and a wife. Your heart is full of fear and insecurity, and no amount of reassurance on my part will ever change that. You have denied this before, but if it weren't true you would not speak the cruel words to people you care about in order to deflect the focus away from you and your errors and instead try to tear the other person down.

I am a good person, I am loyal, strong, loving, brave, and generous—all things you long to be but cannot. I believe that is partially why you have chosen someone else (T.) who is equally selfish, needy, and so desperate to be accepted and loved that you will betray your very families, your morals, your dignity, everything, to have the emptiness filled in your hearts. I would say you both are disgusting people, because genuinely, I am revolted by both of you—but the revulsion is balanced by pity, especially for you F. because you had an opportunity to be with someone who loved you and accepted you and whose heart burst with love for you every day, twenty times a day—but who asked for something from you which you could never truly give—honesty and genuineness. You thought my love for you was based on the image you projected—but I saw you F.—and I loved you completely, purely and eternally. I didn't love you in spite of everything that you found weak and bad about yourself, I loved you in part because of it—it is what makes you human and vulnerable and allows for true intimacy between two people.

Sadly, because you judge yourself so harshly you judged me as well and that is ultimately what killed the love between us. This marriage ending is truly your loss and my gain because it allows me the opportunity to find a man who will look at me and smile, who will kiss me back when I kiss him, who will pull me to him rather than hold me at a distance. (Did you think I never noticed how you always put your hands on the front of my hips with just enough pressure to keep a bit of distance between us when we kissed? Or how you often looked down and away when I told you I loved you and kissed you rather than at me and into me?) I do deserve more than that, I asked for it from you and I gave it to you, but in the end you got the best of yourself and I was betrayed.

What survives between us is our son, our memories, and our friendship. In many ways I would like to be able to walk away from you and heal myself in solitude away from you, and in some ways I am glad that I can't. I do wish you the best, and that is why I don't wish you happiness with a selfish and self destructive whore. Just as my heart was stolen by you, yours was stolen by her and as a result we will always have a blind spot—I for you and you for her. The difference between us now is that I am reclaiming my heart as my own and beginning to take care of it and to care for it myself. I hope that one day you can calm your fears and do the same.

I am beginning to realize the necessity of actively loving myself, of claiming my own self respect, and as a result the respect of others.

J.—as the future is unknown, if I am regretting the loss of this marriage or in a position where we are considering reconciliation—RUN! RUN AS FAST AS I CAN! F. has shown you who he really is—BELIEVE HIM. He only wants you back because of the baby and he is lonely, likely because things aren't working out for him. He will never see you as beautiful, strong, intelligent and as the most valuable person in his life, thusly the person you are. He will always look back at her and long for her, believing she is his true love, despite her betrayals and abandonments and capacity for destroying all that is good in him. He will never look at you as the person he will choose above all others—you will always be his second choice, the one who is there and available. You lied to yourself and convinced yourself that this was untrue before, and the truth came out and you were almost destroyed. Be true to yourself and remember that your love is not second best. You deserve to be first choice, to be loved, to be made love to, to see a glow in someone's eyes that says you are special, loved and perfect to that person. F. is NOT THAT PERSON. You spent 13 years waiting and hoping to see that in him and never really did. Don't let it break your heart, let it make you determined to find that and never settle for less than that in a partner. You will find love, because you are lovable. Don't let him hurt you again, because he will. He doesn't love you the way you need to be loved, and never will. It is time to let your demons be vanquished, to look towards the future and smile, to look back at the past and glow because you are wiser and stronger than you would have ever been otherwise. Some loves have to end, and this was one of them. I don't fully believe this now—but hopefully the future me will.

Love Always,

J.

WRITTEN: December 28, 2005
SENT: November 13, 2006

Dear FutureMe,

I'm writing to you because I don't have an old friend to talk to today. C. and I were together last night. We lay all but naked on my loft. He wanted to do things I'd never done and I'd pull his hand away or say "stop—just not right now"—but he kept trying and eventually I just let him. I told him he could touch but I didn't want him to look. He said "don't be

shy, don't be emberressed—I want to help you be comfortable with yourself." I had asked him before we did anything if he will regret it later—he
said no. He put his hands down my pants. I felt him too. Later, he said he
had to go so his roommates wouldn't be suspicious. He scrunched up his
face and said he felt guilty and he hoped I felt guilty too. I said I've never
been with a guy who didn't feel guilty. I told him I didn't want him to
leave because I'd be alone. "look—maybe I should explain to you where I
stand on these things" "no no I understand—" I interrupted. "I'm a christian and—" he continued. I wondered if he knew what a hypocrite he was
making of himself saying that. "look, I've been here before. I understand."
I said to him. This was all too familiar from D. He fumbled around for
his clothes. "are you ok?" he asked, halfway out the door. "yeah."

Maybe it was too much too fast. I guess we went physically where we
weren't emotionally.

He called me Mary.

WRITTEN: February 05, 2006
SENT: February 05, 2007

Dear FutureMe,

I am on the phone with A. currently. Do you remember her? I am talking
in an odd accent.

Do you remember all those times we used to watch Veggie Tales sing
along together? with A.? A. W? A. Frou Frou Dinoggin?

Hmm. I wonder when I am going to send this. Will I get this a year from
now? A week? Two days? 70 years? What to decide. Hmm.

"Mullets are bad. If in the future you think they're good, just look at this e-mail to remind you that they're not."

Do you remember you thought you would never get through that report last night? Well, you did. Brokeback Mountain is the devil's film. And if you're wondering where all the cowboys have gone it's there.

Mullets are bad. If in the future you think they're good, just look at this e-mail to remind you that they're not.

Have you ever wondered why devil's food cake is called "Devil's" food cake? And why it tastes better? Is it implying that sin is more fun than salvation? I think so.

I should learn how to play my guitar. If you haven't done it by now, you should. Really. Go. Now.

I'm most definitely going to a Studio C on Sunday. Who loves the Fray? I do. Did anyone else see that Fabio commercial during the Super Bowl? Yeah—how scary was that? "Shampoo d'italia." No, thanks.

Yeah, yesterday was the Super Bowl, if you didn't get that. Hopefully you aren't reading this in the morning.

Guess what? Chicken butt.

Love to myself,
Me

WRITTEN: February 06, 2006
SENT: October 31, 2006

Dear FutureMe,

Do you remember today? Have you forgotten yourself already?

You were miserable at your job—your editor snapped at you and you still haven't had a chance to write a decent sentence since November—yet you decided to turn down another job offer. It was the tedium that persuaded you. No need to trade one tedium for another.

Once you made the decision, there was that sinking feeling again. Trapped. Stuck in that office, staring out the window at busy-looking people disappearing into the bowels of Big Government, while you're suffocating inside with your wilting potted plants and stacks of papers and dreams of great prose. Hot steamy Dragonwell tea is the highlight of the day lately.

Things will get better, won't they? Haven't heard back from that other job—the real one, with the kindly editor—which means you weren't right for that one, either. Trapped here instead.

> **"Maybe what I'm most afraid of is true: My enthusiasm far outstrips my talent."**

Maybe what I'm most afraid of is true: My enthusiasm far outstrips my talent. I hate people like that. They break my heart, and I pity them, and I don't ever want to be one of them.

So have I become that? Have I given up? Please say no. Please be remembering this and wondering how I could have doubted that things would work out in the end, somehow. Please be happy right now.

WRITTEN: December 20, 2005
SENT: December 20, 2006

Happy birthday!!! Hey girl … you probably forgot all about this email you are sending to yourself. But here you go—surprise! Enjoy … this is your birthday gift to yourself. Remember the memories of the ohhh sooo unforgettable L.??? Before I forget, here are some questions!!! Did you finally get over him? What did you learn? Are you in love? Do you still think you are depressed? Have you had sex with another man other than L.? Have you had sex with L. after he took your virginity? I really hope you are finally a happy person … satisfied with life and appreciative of everything you do have … because you have a lot. I love you … hehe. I love myself.

I spoke to M. over the phone today. He was so drunk so, of course, he told me way too much information, but because he was drunk, I know it was all true. Thanks, M. for being such an asshole and thank you for teaching me that men are truly stupid. Thanks for telling me about L. and how much of a big asshole he is (even bigger than you). Now I have made up my mind. No more thinking about L.! No more! But how will I do that? I think about him everyday. I mean Every. Single. Day. In my literature class, I participated to read an excerpt from a book only because it mentioned a guy named M. and I wanted to say his name out loud in front of everyone in lecture. I wanted to pronounce every syllable of his name as if he was sitting right next to me. Why did he change so suddenly? Sometimes people don't know how much they hurt others, but that's ok. I guess this is just another life lesson I have been taught. I just have to figure out exactly what that lesson was.

WRITTEN: December 24, 2005
SENT: December 22, 2006

Future:

Have you done anything worthwhile? Cured cancer? Created a unified field theory? Been into space? Written the Great American Novel?

I thought not. I'm so disappointed in you.

-Past

WRITTEN: July 04, 2006
SENDING: April 08, 2018

4296 days

Dear FutureMe,

On this day you vandalized a car with A. You spent the night in jail and got bonded out the next day for $1,000. Your trial was on Aug 28th. Hopefully you didn't get that felony and hopefully your still friends with A. or maybe more.

Your a SENIOR!!! whoo hoo!!!! Its great cuz theres no doubt in your mind that your gonna graduate. You've thought about dropping out but not seriously. Your reasons are cuz you don't want to get out of bed thats why. It has nothing to do with grades or peers or anything serious. You haven't decided if you want to go to college or not. People keep asking you if your gonna go or what you want to be. You dont know nor have the money. You either want to be a chef or own a pet shop from the opinion of your friends. After watching Hells Kitchen your not sure you want that kind of pressure. Your not good at math or being a leader so your not sure if you can run a business. Hey! Maybe you could be a breeder and let your spouse be the money maker.

But you'll keep thinking "what if?" Jus try a junior college or something. It wouldnt hurt. Your deff gonna need a job. But where? You could always work with B. at Walmart, maybe get A. to come along too. Good luck, love you.

WRITTEN: August 15, 2006
SENT: July 24, 2007

Dear FutureMe,

1 month, every month, until it sticks … remember:

1) Your job does not make you cool, don't spend so much time on it.

> "Being the best at something you hate is like winning a lifetime supply of KFC."

2) You have lived with less money before and you were no less happy—sometimes you were happier.

3) Make decisions based on your whole life—being the best at something you hate is like winning a lifetime supply of KFC—unlimited amounts of bad-for-you food that you do not like is no prize.

4) Happiness for you is finding ways to direct your creative energy into experiences for your and others to enjoy—the more time you do this, the better everything will be. Have a party, go to a party, open a bar, open a hair salon. Being a good business lady does not mean making money for other people is your destiny.

5) Don't start being afraid of being unconventional now, being unconventional is how you got here—let it take you someplace better, it is not the time to hedge your bets.

WRITTEN: January 10, 2006
SENT: February 10, 2006

Dear FutureMe,

While I am struggling to grasp the concept of adulthood, I'm sure you've got it all figured out. Right now, I'm a recent college grad with a mountain of credit card debt, trying to figure out how a 3.8 GPA helps me in the real world. While I'm not exactly looking forward to getting older, I am looking forward to figuring out life.

I hope your first year at the job I'm about to start has been good. You are still there, aren't you? It is your seventh job in two years and I hope you're not on number eight.

Yesterday I decided to start a wine cellar, and bought the first bottle, which supposedly will be much better 5 years from now. It's strange buying a bottle of wine and thinking that I won't drink it until I'm 30. So, how's that cellar coming along? Do you have more than one bottle? Do you even still have the one?

I've got a beautiful tattoo in progress, and I'm doing a nude photo shoot in a couple weeks when it's done. I hope you like the tattoo and the photos. I wouldn't do this stuff if I thought you wouldn't.

Love,
Your 25-year-old self

WRITTEN: March 16, 2006
SENT: March 16, 2007

Dear FutureMe,

Today I am pathetic. Hopefully I'm better off when you read this again. I'm like 4 days from my medical boards and I'm freaking out and expressing it terribly. I have begun to drink, smoke, and have unprotected sex with a person who is not my boyfriend. So, I'm probably going to have to break it off with him soon too. Basically I'm spiraling downward. So this is not going to be pleasant to read. It's christmas eve and I'm alone in Ohio throwing a pity party for myself.

"I can barely remember who I am."

Let's see, I've lost 5 lbs, which is normally a good thing, but now not so much since it's just because I've turned into such a basket case that I can barely eat. My whole sense of self, determination, morality, everything is unreachable. I can barely remember who I am. Thankfully, I know as soon as the boards are over these terrible feelings will pass, and hopefully within the 3 weeks I have off I will have achieved some kind of grasp on getting myself back. So, future self I don't ask much of you, as I am not in much of a position to expect anything,

34

but by the time you read this I'm hoping that you will have quit smoking, tempered the drinking and hopefully gone permanently celibate. Maybe not permanent, but at least for a little while until you get a grip.

You are smart and you are strong so you don't need the mental crutches that those things provide. Work hard, help others and make the world take notice of you, because you are spectacular! Pain only builds character, so by the time you get this you ought to be an icon. Madonna & Britney watch yourselves! haha. Oh yeah, you from the past, you were an idiot but you were marginally funny too. Hope you keep that trait. Take care.

~A withered, sloppy, messy you

WRITTEN: December 24, 2005
SENT: January 24, 2006

Dear FutureMe,

Its Christmas Eve 2005. You're sitting here in your bathroom of your small condo, the dog is sleeping on his back with his paws in the air. You're listening to Let's Get Lifted by John Legend. It's been quite a year for you. You began the year on unemployment, wondering if you'd ever find a job or find your way. And then you decided to go to Grad school. Took the plunge, took out the loans, and just did it. So full time work in insurance and full time grad school can tend to put a little strain on the day to day activities and a serious relationship. And then there was that phone call on a random Wednesday night in June—when the supposed love of your life says "I'm moving out. I don't love you anymore" and you were broken and sad and didn't want to get out of bed, live in the condo anymore, keep the dog, etc etc.

But you kept going to school, you kept living life—and now you've traveled a lot and done so many things he probably would have held you back from. You've danced with cute guys, traveled to Italy, Martha's Vineyard, you're going to So. America, and you're going skiing without him. And you're strong. No matter what you are thinking right now—this whole year has made you stronger than ever. In the future—are you going to be married to an Italian chef? Did you get up the courage to ask that old high school friend out? Are you an aunty? Did you finally get your masters? Are you making mucho money doing private practice? Did you get burnt out? Do you still listen to Marc Broussard? Are you still scared to drive in the stupid snow? Did you ever learn to play more than three chords? Do you still think that being 26 years old is old?? Do you still talk to T. your long lost pen pal? Did you guys ever meet up? Did you friend make it back from Afghanistan in one piece?

There's so many questions I have about the future—I just hope I'm happy!! I want to write a book—have I done that yet? I want to have kids—do I have those? I want to fall in love with someone who will love me forever—not just conditionally and then leave me for some desperate older woman. ugh.

I hope in years from now this is going to seem like such a joke and I'll realize he did me a big favor. Merry Christmas, G.

WRITTEN: December 24, 2005
SENT: December 24, 2006

Dear FutureMe,

Ive just worked my first week at hartmans kosher butcher shop. Just my luck they were just changeing everything over for passover, I had no idea glatt kosher rules were so complicated! Its kind of funny, not only am I the only one working there who doesnt speak hebrew, I'm not even jewish. Im surprised they were allowed to hire me. Still the money is nothing to sneeze at—$10/hr for getting people steaks and roasts form behind the counter. Its not the best wages, but most counter help in this city pulls in minnimum wage. The only downside is I have a rash on my hands from handeling the salted meat and my right wrist is killing me because I pulled it the first day :-(

This week I worked 48.5 hours, $485 a week isn't bad for a chick with a crewcut, fresh out of high school.

WRITTEN: March 25, 2006
SENT: March 25, 2007

Dear FutureMe,

Yesterday J. came home at 10 am. I figured she had been at L.'s house even after she swore she wouldnt be over there anymore. She said she was at L.'s, I asked 'what were you doing?' She said trying to figure out what to do with her life. I asked then if she had sex with him and coldly she said Yes. I asked if she loved him and she said Yes. I asked if she was leaving and she said Yes. We kind of sat there for awhile. I wanted to throw up. She put her hand on my leg and it felt so dirty I told her not to touch me. She got her things and I had A. from upstairs take her to the guys house. I was a drama queen and got rid of all the myspace friends I had, I might log in as her and delete all my friends from her profile. Yea Im doing that now. My mind keeps racing, Im in shock still. I should have seen it coming but I never figured she would cheat. At least she told me right after so I didn't have to touch her. I've starting my fasting of course. Water and cigarettes for me. You really need to stop smoking. I'm going to try and make it to church this week.

This is a very difficult time for me. I hope by this time next year you can have some things sorted out. And quit smoking, it's our body you are ruining. I weigh my normal 160 right now and have decided to no longer use any illegal drugs. Hopefully I will stick with that. I don't know if I want to stay in Seattle now, I dont know if I can take running into them. After 7 years you think you know a person. I'm going to go to take a long long shower and wash away the filthiness and then shave my head. I'm going to look like a nazi camp victim but it's fine.

2006 is supposed to be my year. I sure hope it was. I hope you are eating better than I am right now. Go get yourself a slice of pizza and think of me who can not eat. This is day 2 of not eating. Maybe ill write again later to keep you posted. I think I might. This has been a tough year. I thought last year was the worst.

WRITTEN: December 19, 2005
SENT: December 19, 2006

Dear FutureMe,

It's Friday, 11:37 am, the night before New Year's Eve, and you're at work, but unable to really concentrate. You've been thinking all week about S., hoping he'd call while he was away (he didn't, or hasn't yet) and that he'd be back in time to spend New Year's Eve with you (doubtful, but maybe you were pleasantly surprised). I know how much you hope he will. Expectations suck, don't they? They only lead to disappointment.

> **"Expectations suck, don't they? They only lead to disappointment."**

A year or two from now, when you get this email, he will likely only have been a blip in your life. A short respite in your years of solitude. Maybe you're married, maybe not. I've been wrong about that before. Are your loved ones telling you not to be so picky? Tell them to bite me, or you, whoever. Remember that you deserve someone great, someone who will love you unconditionally, (and as I know you I know that you're also thinking/hoping S. is the one who will do that) so, if it hasn't happened, don't be too hard on yourself. Don't blame God, or your reserved nature. You are who you are and to be someone else will only get you an unhappy life and a divorce.

You rock and even if you don't find someone who thinks you're amazing and appreciates the finer points of your personality you will always have you, and hopefully a dog.

Love,
PastMe

WRITTEN: December 30, 2005
SENDING: December 30, 2008

Dear FutureMe,

Dear future me. Happy 30th Birthday. And if you're reading this, it means that the world hasn't ended. Though probably, the US is at war somewhere in the middle east, and maybe … in North Korea. If in your time, the US is fighting China, then say goodbye to everything you love cause it's fucking over.

But if there is relative peace, I am surprised and happy for you. How is your career going? Because today, as I write this to you, it's the most important thing to me. Is it fear or just ambition that drives me so I often wonder? Is it true passion, what I feel, or just a desire to make myself feel like my life is meaningful? By now you should know, and I hope that there is more happiness than regret in your life because you were un-happy for so long and it would be a shame if that were the case again now.

But in any case, despite your best efforts, you've probably made a mistake or two between now and where you are. I can't predict the future, but I hope that whatever injury you suffered was worth it and made you a better person.

Do you still like The Killers? Phoenix? The Postal Service? Or have they passed out of your life? Music is always dated. Like for instance, I had unconditional love for third eye blind, until I turned 22. Something happened and suddenly, their music represented an era of my life that was passed. I could no longer relate to either the time period or the music that defined it. Has that happened yet? I expect so. In fact, I expect that you listen to music less often. You should be busy, too busy with work and career to care about music.

Where are you living? At 25 you hated Los Angeles and dreamt of living abroad. If you forget why you never took off, it's because you were much too committed to establishing yourself here. You told yourself you could not live with yourself if you ran away for the purpose of adventure. You wanted to make something of yourself. You had the hardest time earning respect not from friends or lovers or peers but from yourself. Why were you always so ashamed of your past, and the mistakes you made?

Do you still love poetry? I don't read much, fiction like much of life has become a bore. The only time really you feel anything is poetry or film. Is that still the case?

Who is left in your life these days? Here I am twenty five

> **"The facade has become prettier by practice and practicality, but underneath it's still quite ugly. I am an ugly person, always have been."**

years old and already so many people whom were close are strangers now. I should expect worse. I have not become warmer over the years. The facade, the public face has become prettier by practice and practicality, but underneath it's still quite ugly. I am an ugly person, always have been. Who are your friends? Have you retained any? Do you feel alone, and if so, do you believe that is the price you pay for your success?

At twenty I could not imagine marriage. But at fifteen, I could not imagine being twenty-five. Nor at twenty. Are you in love? Is love still possible? I predict that you're married or very single. You have little passion for women at 25, but maybe that's just a condition of your disinterest with people in general. Are you still hateful or has it developed into something like mild indifference? I hope that latter because all that hate you had made you a miserable human being.

Where is J.? Have things become ruined between you and her? You didn't think it was possible for someone to chase away so many lovers in a single lifetime but were you wrong. You made a lot of promises to her. I hope you kept your word.

Honestly, I hope everything I dreamt of came true. I hope in the years since we last met, you've continued to work hard. I hope you have not lost focus or desire, and have stayed the course. I know life can be difficult, and you felt for a long time you were becoming colder, less human, but in the end, that was the only way you do make something of yourself. Look around you, this is not the life you want for the future. Nothing comes without cost my friend.

In the chance, however, that you are not the person you dreamt of becoming, that the life you possess is not the one your heart designed then I am sorry. Don't look back in anger, just know that you did the very best you could and that is all anyone, including you, could ask.

Despite my concerns, the future looks bright. I hope at 30 you are still independent and strong and have passion for justice and fairness and speaking for the underspoken. I still hope family is your priority, I hope you still believe in loyalty. I hope that even if you relent much, you retain your values and the heart of yourself. Try not to be so sad about the past, it's not as good as you chose to remember.

WRITTEN: September 07, 2006
SENDING: September 13, 2010

Dear FutureMe,

I hope that this is an unnecessary message. I hope that things have worked themselves out by the time you read this. But I have to admit, I'm not that hopeful.

If he's still being selfish—if he's still thinking of himself before anyone else, if he's still sitting on his ass on the couch with a beer and a video game, then it's time to do something about it.

You deserve better. Right now, I'm trying to give him space and let him find whatever it is he lost. I know it's not easy for him, and I don't want to make any decisions when I'm so emotional. I pray that he has found it by the time this hits your in box.

> **"Today is the day you decided that love may not be enough."**

If he hasn't, then I tell you this: Today, December 23rd 2005, is the day you decided that love may not be enough. And you decided to give him some more time, and to try and help in whatever way you can.

But if it doesn't work...if he doesn't wake up...if he isn't the person you fell in love with, well...then it's time to end it.

It's going to hurt. It's not going to be easy. You're going to second guess yourself and you're going to want to run back.

Don't do it.

Stop putting your life on hold for other people. In ten years, you don't want to be looking back and thinking what a waste it all was.

WRITTEN: December 23, 2005
SENT: December 23, 2006

Dear Myself,

Have you and R. slept together yet? At this time, 12/24/05, you haven't but have sent some pornographic emails to each other. You've kissed, pretty damn passionately, and got a wonderful feel of her breast and her fine ass. She seems like she's horny for you but being as how she's married for years and so are you it's a question. Also, if for some reason you're not together in some way, she's the first black woman you ever kissed. You're an assistant at the Big Box at home now and have thought seriously about going to Canada to work. How'd that go? When you read this your daughter should be 22 and your son 16. She was a handful and rebellious and was so in love with M. He was just getting that way but was a real comedian. You're pretty unhappy with your marriage, your wife spends money all the time, is fat as hell, and not very sexually appealing. I hope I, meaning you, have made some changes and ARE living with R., maybe married. I think she's really a great woman, intelligent, and VERY sexy.

WRITTEN: December 24, 2005

SENDING: December 24, 2010

So he's coming down tomorrow. Excited? Or secretly dreading it?

Prepare yourself, but don't overdo it. Try to be natural, be yourself. He'll probably know if you're not acting like yourself that it's just nerves, but still, do your best. And be patient with him, too. He's never done this before either.

Breathe. Just keep breathing. You love each other for who you are, and while there may be some slight initial setbacks when you see each others' real appearances, mannerisms, and the like, remember that inside there is a man whom you love very much, and that you'll get used to it.

Remember to dig out your discount/coupon book—it's all good through May at least, and some of the stuff could be really useful, like discount movie rentals and food and stuff. Oh, and even bowling, or whatever movie's in the Gallagher Thursday. You should probably go look that up, by the way. The coupon book's in the top drawer of your desk.

Also remember to get some good sleep, and set your alarm. Last thing you want to do is oversleep and keep him waiting while you hurriedly throw yourself together. I understand that it may be hard to sleep, especially considering your usual method of getting to it, but you do your best, okay? Even grab some PM medicine if you need it. You need your rest.

And stop worrying! He loves you, and that's not going to change any time soon.

WRITTEN: January 15, 2006
SENT: March 03, 2006

Dear FutureMe,

Um yeah, you USED to put pennies on the ground for people (mostly little kids) to pick up and have a nice day. Don't stop doing that.

-you

WRITTEN: November 10, 2005
SENT: January 01, 2006

Dear FutureMe,

I am a cynical pessimist who hates everyone and believes that they are all out to get me and jealous, too. Riley is four and talks back. I still hate my father. I have no health insurance.

WRITTEN: September 09, 2003
SENT: February 28, 2007

Dear FutureMe,

Did I do what was right? Did I accomplish what you wanted to accomplish? Have you fulfilled my potential? Does it matter? Were you right all along or has everything changed? I wish you could tell me which thing I was supposed to focus on. I hope I haven't fucked you over by picking the wrong things, or the right things in the wrong sequence. Do you feel like a failure? Do you feel trapped? If so, it's my fault, and I'm sorry. I must've zigged when I should've zagged. Life is cold and hard. But is it empty? I don't know, but I think you do. I hope you're in love. Forgive me for everything I've done wrong. I was weak.

> "Do you feel like a failure? Do you feel trapped? If so, it's my fault, and I'm sorry. I must've zigged when I should've zagged."

WRITTEN: November 07, 2005
SENDING: January 01, 2010

Dear FutureMe,

This is kind of weird … do you remember doing this, but with real letters—like from that church camp that you so hated? Now I can do it with e-mails … isn't that fun.

So, you're depressed and lonely right now. The people you live with left you and went to a concert, so you're sitting there in your underwear wishing that someone liked you enough to come over and keep you company.

But no one does. It figures.

You hate your best friends right now, but you're stuck with them until, basically, you can get out of that little burg you call home and get away from that god-forsaken place. You daren't tell them … their feelings might get hurt.

But what you're really afraid of.

The REAL reason you don't tell them … is that you're afraid that their feelings WON'T get hurt … and that would be worse than any feeling on this planet.

So you keep it to yourself.

You're keeping a lot to yourself these days … fighting bulimia and self-injuring urges, violent and harmful images going through your head … does that still happen? Do you still think about how it would feel to kill someone or watch someone die? Or even just hear their screams as they were maimed and tortured? Do you think of all the different ways you could die

"Have you changed? Somehow I doubt it."

and not get blamed for suicide? Because you sure as hell used to, even inadvertently, and it scared the shit out of you.

Everyone you have ever cared about has left you because you're fat, ugly, and clingy.

Have you changed?
Somehow I doubt it.
Maybe someday you'll find comfort and peace.
Or maybe you'll just die young or kill yourself.
Either way.

WRITTEN: November 06, 2005
SENT: November 06, 2006

Dear FutureMe,

I am sitting at work with nothing to do because I don't have envelopes to label at the moment. I have not paid my rent yet, for some reason, and I may be evicted because of it. I don't know. I don't have the money. I am also going on a kind of date tonight with S., even though I am currently sleeping with H., a girl who routinely dumps me. Christmas is in 5 days. So! What are you doing right now? Is this Christmas going to be a bit better? I did get a bonsai tree from H. How is it doing now, anyway? Dead? A work of art? I'm curious how you did taking care of it. Anyway, I guess you'll never write me back, but that's okay! I know I'm way harder to get a hold of than you.

WRITTEN: December 20, 2005
SENT: December 20, 2006

OK shit head this is a wake up call if you are still on probation, still with out a license, and still owe restitution, WTF do you think you are doing? STOP spending money on booze, put that money on what you owe and for the classes. Granted its only a 6 pack or something but think once we get off probation you can do what ever you want. I am giving you a timeline, I know that you dont ever seem to do things the way you should so you have 18 mos to get this done, and if not (I will hold you to this) you MUST SELL YOUR 1968 FORD MUSTANG to the first buyer to pay for what ever you owe money to.

I know it hurts to write this and I am hoping that it doesnt come down to this I … WE love this car, so dont let it go. Pull your head out of your ass … Get off this stuff, it has lost you a really good girl I am hoping R. has never married but you win and lose some and she was lost due to your alcohol problem stop cheating on your GF she is a good one granted she needs to lose weight but she is truly repentent for what she did so GET OVER IT.

WRITTEN: January 04, 2006
SENDING: May 25, 2008

Dear FutureMe:

This is an e-mail you remind yourself what you were like a year ago today. If you remember today exactly, you had a doctor's appointment today to check up on the heart surgery you had.

These days you are concerned with your credit score and you really want to buy a house. Your score now is 561. What is it now? Has it improved any? You are also waiting for a kidney transplant. How is that going?

You are single now and the closest thing you have to a girlfriend is your friend's wife. Have you messed around with her anymore? You made some New Years resolutions, how's that going? You said you were going to be 180 lbs by this time. You also said you were going to try to start a business making something with your hands. Did you ever end up going back to school? Did you ever ask that recruiter T. out? Do you remember her? She was HOT!!! Speaking of hot girls, what ever happened to N.? Did you stop talking to her like you said? And did you ever go see C.? Hmmm. Is there anything else that I want to remind you of? Not really. You are doing good today, relieved that you are okay from your heart surgery and by the time you receive this e-mail, you should be 100% better than you are today.

Here's hoping to a fantastic 2006!!!

Your buddy,
PastMe

WRITTEN: December 20, 2005
SENT: December 20, 2006

Dear FutureMe,

I think the problem with this whole FutureMe thing is that it focuses much more on the end result than the process. I could ask you if you have moved on, if you are happy, if you feel alive, but I am forgetting that who I am now must be the catalyst to change things. So, I won't ask if you are over T. or if you still cringe when A. speaks in English class because I can't see a change in two months.

But the purpose of this e-mail was to make you feel warm on the anniversary of the descent. And I know I won't let this e-mail or the day slip my mind, but I would love to think you can slip underneath it. Let it gently float over you.

Pray for me. Because your past selves never disappear, they just manifest themselves into ghosts that'll haunt you later.

"I could ask you if you are happy, if you feel alive, but I am forgetting that who I am now must be the catalyst to change things."

WRITTEN: September 26, 2005
SENT: October 26, 2005

Dear FutureMe,

Yes, you are 25. Yes, I am 15. I wonder firstly if you'll get this. Are you dead? Has your email changed? Has this been marked as spam?

I've sent you so many emails that over the next half of your lifetime you will get many a random rambling. But worse, they are all questions about the future. So let me tell you about the present.

You have this very year grown up. 'Tis true. This year you became a man. You're still a virgin, sadly, passing up a chance to sleep with your [now ex-] girlfriend due to your petty morals and such. But you've grown up and won't let that get in your way; you'll make it very clear you'll have a girlfriend for little other reason than sex.

Sex aside, you are speeding through high school. This year you are completing your sophomore, junior, and senior year(!). Hopefully by the time you get this such news will be menial, as I will have done all kinds of other extraordinary things.

Right now, you are dedicating your life to training to join the CIA. You aren't under official training because it's illegal at your age, but you're speeding through school, doing weight training, teaching yourself new languages, studying psychology, and desensitizing yourself in hopes of becoming the perfect machine by the time you're 18.

So what now? Are you in the CIA now? Has this email just blown your cover in some operation you've been a part of for several years?

That thought amuses and terrifies me. To think the youthful I would be the demise of the the older I.

But what if you're not in the CIA? What are you doing? You terrify me, FutureMe.

Perhaps you've made some friends. You've moved out of this godforsaken East Coast town and moved somewhere foreign, lavishing yourself in women and luxury as you make international deals worth millions. I know I could do it. I'm already making obscene amounts of money for someone my age, and legally at that.

For now, I do absolutely nothing. I pass the time, caught in limbo between childhood and adulthood. And with passing the time comes the reflections and fears, thus producing such emails as these.

At the moment, I have so many ambitions that it seems impossible for me to fail. If you're working a minimum wage job, still living with your parents, I hope you have the decency to escape and live your life as a bum somewhere. At least there would be some pride in that.

And if you're in the aforementioned situation, this email has probably ruined your day. A nostalgic look into yesteryear, perhaps observing the naive notions of a 15-year-old who considers himself a man and above most of his peers.

Have you toned down your arrogance? Do you still consider your ego an asset? At the moment, you are probably condescending without realizing it, certainly egotistical. But that's a good thing; if I wasn't egotistical, I wouldn't have attempted most of the things I've accomplished. I don't know if I should write in first or second person.

Bah. I can only hope this email reaches you, for I am spending precious sleeping time to write it. School starts in five hours; I awake in four.

Good luck to you.
PastMe

WRITTEN: January 09, 2006
SENDING: January 09, 2017

Dear FutureMe,

Well you are thirty years old today. Hopefully you have your own home and a good job now? Or perhaps you finally made that move to Mt. Carmel that you had been contemplating. I would guess that C. is gone by now, which is of course hard to imagine in 2006. Or have you somehow managed to walk away from all of that and go on with the rest of life, pretending that you were not forever changed by your involvement with the Branch Davidians and the message that David Koresh taught?

WRITTEN: January 02, 2006
SENDING: September 24, 2010

Dear FutureMe,

I know this email isn't going to mean anything to you unless it has some info about myself, here in October 2005, but all I can think about is stuff I'd like to ask you.

The whole concept of wishing I could ask you stuff is kind of stupid, when you think about it. Ultimately, it's going to be up to me to create my own future; asking you about it feels more like a decision to believe in fate. Or to just give up and let things happen the way they happen. I have a feeling that however my future turns out is going to be affected by chance quite a bit, but I also know that I am capable of just about anything if I really think it's necessary.

I guess the only thing I should worry about is the possibility of getting stuck, like if I have to work full time at a job I hate and I can't quit because I had a kid or something. I'll try not to do anything like that. It's really disturbing to me that there is always the possibility for something I can't control to permanently screw up my life; for a long time I kind of tried not to admit it. I'd see people suffering on the news and my gut reaction would be that they must have been stupid somehow, they must have made a decision sometime that limited their options and allowed them to get trapped (in a hurricane, in a terrorist bomb, etc) but of course that's bull. Sometimes things just happen to people, things that couldn't be prevented, and that scares the crap out of me. But that's an extreme example.

> "Ultimately, it's going to be up to me to create my own future; asking you about it feels more like a decision to believe in fate."

54

On the other end of the spectrum, I suppose there are people who go through life and never get trapped. They're probably the offspring of rich people. I guess I'm learning that most people are somewhere in between, I just have the feeling that I'm closer to the no-options end of the spectrum than the other end. It probably is related to money, and since I have none, it feels that way. Imagine if I couldn't be living at home right now, and couldn't get student loans for college in a year or so—I would really have no assets, and I would also be really trapped. I'd have to work full time at some crap job like Sears and do nothing more than survive; no hopes, no freedom. I guess I just have to figure out how my one real asset, a college degree, is going to give me enough power and choice to work my way up to being independent someday. Or at least happily semi-independent.

I hope when you read this someday you'll be laughing at how stressed out I was about nothing. Or at least feel a sense of relief that things turned out well. Thanks for listening.

WRITTEN: October 01, 2005
SENT: October 01, 2007

Dear FutureMe,

Well, you spent many years worrying too much, even though your rational mind told you that worrying never affected a change. You had a sleep disorder that was nothing less than pure hell. In fact, it rendered you a nervous, miserable wreck. Finally you snapped! There was no one who even cared.

Then you realized they really didn't matter anyway. Everyone is just living for themselves so you decided you would try your hand at it. You stopped worrying and went back to school at the ripe old age of fifty-four. You stopped worrying about anything. Trouble was, that didn't affect a change either. It only made things worse. You didn't even worry enough to do anything about it when you ran out of money.

Now you can't even buy supplies for your art classes and how are you going to pay the rent? Did you think that money was heaven sent? How are you going to pay the high price of being a fool for so long?

Well, things will get better just you wait and see.

Good Luck!
Your Admiring Self

WRITTEN: September 02, 2006
SENT: September 02, 2007

Dear FutureMe,

I am writing to inform you that according to some online quiz, you are scheduled to die on Friday, June 17th 2050, at the tender age of 61 years old.

On that date, you will most likely die from:
Cancer (13%)
Alcoholism (9%)
Heart Attack (5%)
"Cleaning Your Rifle" (4%)

Sooo … 61 seems like a good age, you never wanted to get that old anyway. Do yourself a favor and BE PREPARED.

WRITTEN: January 03, 2006
SENDING: June 17, 2050

Dear FutureMe,

Are you out of debt? Are you pregnant? Are you back in school? Do you have a house?

If the answer to any of these questions is no, WAKE UP!!! You have been this way for too long now. Get a better job. If the business isn't succeeding by now, it never will. Sell, and use the money for a house. Have some freaking babies already!

On the baby topic … Have you treated your cervical cancer yet? If not, you're going to die. You're only 29.

You have 1 year to accomplish these basic goals, things you originally wanted to do by 25. So get moving! You can't slack off forever.

Good luck with the next year, baby. You'll need it.

WRITTEN: August 03, 2006
SENT: October 11, 2007

> **"I like the idea of you receiving bits of the past piece by piece, rather than in complete detail."**

Dear FutureMe,

I have become completely, though temporarily addicted to talking to you. I like the idea of you receiving bits of the past, piece by piece, rather than in complete detail. I like the fact that you'll have to wait until tomorrow to receive the next message. It might be some trivial concern. Or I might say something very emotional and personal. It might contain the very wisdom you need to get through the day.

I'm starting to become sentimental or reflective, and I know you'll probably find that a bit tedious. I think one of the things that impressed me about many of the "future letters" is how they seem to serve a therapeutic purpose: reminding future selves to get massages, to go out more, to enjoy life, to get work done. Above all, to be happy.

Be happy.

WRITTEN: October 07, 2003
SENT: October 11, 2004

Hey, I'm never going to receive this message because I'm gonna be DEAD!

Hm. That kinda sucks.

WRITTEN: March 14, 2005
SENDING: August 20, 2035

11,116 days

Dear FutureMe,

I am more than a little concerned that at some point in the past, following some sort of self-destructive, non-whimsical impulse I may have sent FutureMe email of an abusive nature to myself. Probably something along the lines of, "There is virtually no chance that you have managed to do any of the stuff you wanted to do, you fucking failure." If this is the case, if you have received something like this, or if you are destined to receive something like this, then I want you to think about why it is so tempting to consider my past self as an object for contempt and my future self as an enemy.

Your concerned friend,
PastSelf

WRITTEN: November 07, 2005
SENT: November 07, 2007

Dear FutureMe,

It's been 5 years…

First, the NOT SO important stuff.

So you did great in 2005. How the heck are your stocks doing now? Today the Dow closed down 2.49 at 10959.87. What's it at now? S&P 500 was up 1.55 at 1287.61 So, now that your rich beyond belief and can afford a second home, a full auto M-16 and own 2 or 3 businesses, what are your plans that I never thought of? Do you have $50K in an account just for fun? Are you teaching people how to get out of debt? You've had 2 Masters degrees for a while now. Are they paying off, or were they a waste of time? Are you working on a PhD yet? Did you leave Texas as planned?

Now for the important stuff. (Print this out and take it with you on your next hunt.)

Are you out hunting elk and enjoying nature and the gifts of God? Are you standing on a mountain, just you and God, watching the sun rise? Are you looking forward to a day of hunting, far away from whatever the world thinks is important now? Your son, M., is not old enough to be there with you yet. Is he back at camp with his mother, A., or somewhere else? Next year he should be about the right age to start hunting. Is he excited? How long have you been fishing together now? Does his mother fish with you sometimes? How much time do the three of you make to just go out in the woods, mountains, wherever, and just be together? Is it enough? How often do the three of you watch the sun rise and set. How many campfires have you sat around lately? Do you have a good place for your 16" telescope, 100 miles in the middle of nowhere? When you watch the sun set today, what will God say to you? What will you say to Him? M. has just started to say "I love you, Daddy." What kind of things do you talk about now? Pack a lunch tomorrow and go out into the woods with M. Don't take one single electronic device. Teach him to be a real man who understands the value of life. Teach him how money is just a sideshow to the real life he has before him. Show him the value of just walking alone in nature with nothing but a backpack. I know this e-mail is late. I know you have already done these things. I just wanted to remind you of when you planned them.

WRITTEN: January 13, 2006

SENDING: January 13, 2011

> "How many campfires have you sat around lately?"

60

Dear FutureMe,

Remember that night you talked and talked and talked to P.? How happy you were? That was tonight.

Never ever forget how you felt that night. No matter what happens, if Ohio drains the life out of you, if promises to yourself have been broken, NEVER forget this simple joy.

Someone thinks you are beautiful, inside and out. Someone once said your name with breathless perfection.

Don't ever forget.

WRITTEN: May 21, 2006
SENT: November 21, 2007

549 days

Dear FutureMe,

You've been having a really rough time, you're actually afraid you're going to give up. The 5th was probably the worst day of your life. You have a lot of worst day of your lives now. But the 5th really was one of them. You went to the mall with your best friend M. and her mom to buy M.'s school clothes. You were going to see a movie but did that instead.

Things change. You fell in like again with the most amazing guy. Then made a fool of yourself in front of him. It happens.

> "You fell in like again with the most amazing guy. Then made a fool of yourself in front of him. It happens."

When you came home you told mom what you've wanted to since your cousin has been here. You need to talk alone. Soon. She started to cry. That was probably a bad sign. She sent your cousin out of the room and made you talk. And you talked. And cried. You do that a lot now too. She kept telling you she screwed up everything. She said it in such a way you were so afraid she was going to do something. She said she wanted her kids to have everything she never had as a child. Then she told you something that has probably ruined your life even more. Your mother, the woman who raised you these 17 years (almost 18) told you that your grandpa molested her until she was 16. I almost died. How she can tell me not to tell anyone what she's about to tell me because she's told no one then tell me THAT!?!

You and your dad are the only people who know now that mom told him. You feel so sick all the time thinking about all the times you've been to visit them and given the man who ruined your mom's life a kiss on the cheek. Mom told you he probably doesn't remember. I can't help but think what if he does and he gets some smug sense of satisfaction knowing he's getting away with being a monster?

Don't give up, for your mom's sake.

Love,
You at 17

PS: It's okay to hate him for mom. And try not to throw up or scream and cry when and if you see him.

WRITTEN: August 08, 2005
SENT: August 08, 2006

Dear FutureMe,

Now that I have some time to myself, I have some things to tell you ask you.

1- Did you get the Ferrari or Lamborghini or both?

2- Did Z. grow up? Live thru his teens? Not get killed? Thats ur biggest fear at 35. Your only child getting killed. You know what its like to bury your Mom and Dad and still grieve. Its been 20 years since Mom died and 13 since Dad.

3- Did you ever clean up your act?

4- Did you have a second child? Can you do your self a favore and kind of reflect on the birth, the joys, the sorrows the child/children brought you?

5- Are you and T. still together? Ever "make her an honest woman"?

6- Did man kind ever end war? Ya know in ur youth you were kinda of a war monger. Now that you're a Daddy you pray for Z. to not have to go to war.

7- Hows old man W.? You will never have a friend like him again.

8- Did you become more patient? Happier?

9- Have you learned to love others? Love your self?

Okay on a happier note, T. made 100,000 last year.

You have a Buell, a Harley, a Tiburon, and a Grand Cherokee.

Z. turns 2 in less than 5 days. Remember how scared you were to meet him? Im so glad it worked out well for us.

Its good to be alive, its scary to grow older.

Do me a favor, just kind of sit back, dim the lights and think back and reflect. If you need to cry go ahead. Kiss Z. Kiss the other if there is another. Hug them and please no matter whats happening, tell them you love them. Family is important.

Dont let your self do to your child/children what your Dad did to you. Dont be afraid to say I love you. Dont with hold your emotions if your angry. Dad did that and look what happened. He died the next day. Kiss your self for me.

WRITTEN: January 03, 2006
SENDING: January 03, 2017

Dear FutureMe, hello!

well, last week I had a moment of absolute fear as I was brushing my hair one morning that I am nearly thirty and as yet still unmarried and not participating in climbing any kind of career ladder. the moment passed when I realised that six years off is not 'nearly' by any stretch of the imagination, and rational J. once more regained the control she has so capably and efficiently been exercising for the past few weeks.

however, not two days ago I was horrified to discover …

A GREY HAIR

this is not like the 'grey hairs' my mum delighted finding in my hair when I was 18 whilst we were in the middle of boots shopping in blackpool and shouting 'oo look a grey hair and you're only eighteen' and that upon examination turned out to be blonde. oh no. this was a real grey hair.

so mild panic began to rise, especially as I recently spoke to s. the ex who is having a personal crisis about being thirty in 16 days time, and how he is not where he thought he would be now when he was 20. and I began to wonder about what I expected my life to be like when I am thirty and whether this is realistic or predictable. obviously it isn't the second. in my mind I thought, I'd like to be married to someone christian and intelligent who appreciates the arts and maybe have one child and another in mind. I would like to have pursued the beginnings of an interesting career that I could take up again once my children are at school in a few years time. and I'd like to not be living in fleetwood still. maybe not realistic either. the panic mounts as I realise that six years isn't very long at all to 'achieve' all of these things.

and bear in mind that all the time my house is getting more and more in need of cleaning and tidying and I'm never at home because I'm out virtually every evening spending my time talking to moody, smelly and weird teenagers. if I can't organise my life so that my house is in order, how will I organise myself a husband, kid and career in the next 6 years!!!

so I decided to find a box to empty some drawers to make more room for my socks, and this involved clearing out the cupboard under the stairs (it's amazing how things pile up on you in 12 months) which made me feel much better—having grappled with something monstrous and messy and overcoming it—and helped me find a box. what was in the now new sock drawers were bags and boxes of random bits and pieces that I have kept for years—letters, cinema tickets, teenage diaries, little notes from flatmates—nice things. I had a nice time sorting them all out and found a list I had made right at the end of university.

> "If I can tick three things off my lifetime ambition list in 18 months, then maybe I can expect to be vaguely happy in six years' time."

you may remember because you were there, sitting in the crags and talking about what you would like to do with the rest of our lives—our ambitions and hopes, and A. was talking about how it would 'never be the same again—we'd never be together again—ever ...' anyway I wrote my list (and so did she I think) and this was the list I found—my list of life ambitions. some things are ridiculous e.g. 'live on orkney for a year' 'contribute something meaningful and memorable to society', 'write a novel' etc. but I was very surprised to see that I have already fulfilled three of the things listed on 'My Great List of Lifetime Ambitions'—I have this year (very luckily, I feel) 'visited the Louvre', 'been to New York in the autumn' and 'stood on top of the Empire State Building'.

it cheered me up. if I can tick three things off my lifetime ambition list in 18 months, then maybe I can expect to be vaguely happy in six years' time.

I hope you're feeling happy today—life's not worth panicking about is it? really? think about all the love and friendship you've experienced and thank God!

66

love you lots
your slightly psycho 24 year old self

WRITTEN: December 11, 2003
SENDING: October 05, 2009

Dear 'FutureMe',

This Christmas (2005), I was violently ill after having eaten [brand name] pork, and stayed up half the night in agony because if I curled up in bed I found it impossible to breathe, and so had to sleep flat out on my back. Please don't eat [brand name] pork. Ever.

Love,
'PastMe'

WRITTEN: December 21, 2005
SENT: December 01, 2006

345 days

Dear FutureMe,

This is the anniversary of the day your husband had the worst headache
of his life—a burst aneurism caused a subarachnoid hemorrhage.

Remember the trip to the hospital on Saturday, the stroke he had on
Sunday, the Monday you thought you were a widow for sure. The trip to
Emory, the craniotomy, the coma. The day the doctor told you that he
would never hold a conversation with you again, never live outside a nurs-
ing home. You planned his funeral, called a Unitarian minister you did
not even know, just because you could not see letting your dear husband
go without some ceremony. You ordered clothes for both of you.

Then, just before Christmas, hope! The doctor said, "We do everything
or we do nothing." Naturally, you chose everything, and remember how
happy you were, just that he had a chance? He had improved a bit, and
the doctor told you, "The only way you pull the plug now is if you think
he would not accept less
than a 100 percent recovery."

Remember the gradual
awakening from the coma,
the month you spent sleeping on a foldout chair in
the NICU waiting room.
Remember the families you
met, the bond you shared
with them.

> "Remember the trip to the
> hospital on Saturday, the
> stroke he had on Sunday,
> the Monday you thought
> you were a widow for sure."

Remember how badly you wanted him to go to a rehab hospital in your
home town, and how the human resources person at your work made it
work for you.

Remember the first days at that rehab hospital. Remember how S. and N. and A. and V. were there for both of you in such a big way.

As you write this, he has been weaned off the ventilator. He has a speaking tube in his trach, but is not saying much. He lifted his arm today. You think he is depressed.

So how is life now, a year later? Is he alive? Is he at home? Can he walk, talk, teach? Is he happy?

And how about you, dear one? Have you taken care of yourself? I hope so.

You found courage in yourself you did not know you had. You were brave, you were there, you accepted the support of your friends and you made what, at this point, seem to be the right decisions.

Future me, I hope this finds you both well.

I love you,
Me

WRITTEN: January 15, 2006
SENT: December 03, 2006

Dear FutureMe,

Do you remember, while still in grade school, how your parents went to a party on new years eve, leaving you home alone? You were so lonely and scared you cried, and prayed that God would send someone. Within an hour, at 10 pm, your brother came home from a bar, drunk, and asked why you were up so late? But he had his wristwatch on upside down, and thought it was 3:30 am, that's why he came home when you needed someone?

Do you remember, in high school, when you wanted to meet a girl, and you prayed to God that one would move into the neighborhood, and about 2 weeks later a beautiful girl moved in about 3 houses down, but each day at the bus stop, you were too afraid to talk to her?

Do you remember, in college, when your leather keychain broke, leaving loose keys in your pocket, and you prayed to God for another keychain, and as you walked to class, about half a block up the street, you saw a silver metal ring lying on the sidewalk, and you picked it up, and it was a key ring?

"Do you remember your dreams?"

Do you remember, at age 33, when you were so lonely and depressed you wanted to kill yourself, but decided first to go to the freedom fest music festival, and as the girl on stage fumbled and struggled to play "Crazy on You," you saw a blue flame come out of the clear sky and give the girl the ability to play the song without a flaw?

Do you remember your dreams? The chorus of voices chanting that Latin phrase "Deo Optimo Maximo et in honor Silas…" and that you looked it up on the internet, and found it was written on a stone chapel in England dedicated to casualties of World War I? How did that get in your head?

And that other dream, how the voice behind you said that the world is like an arena, full of tests and battles, with winners and losers? How worry is pointless, because, as nothing more than atoms and molecules, we don't know from where we came, and we cannot know where the future will take us? How the world is filled with hidden dimensions beyond our perception, and we cannot perceive any more than a flatworm can? Do you remember how rested you felt knowing God is in control of everything? Has he not shown himself alive, and isn't he with you now? By the will of the Father you were chosen, and the full personality of God has manifested himself to you. You will remember, so let it be.

WRITTEN: January 18, 2006
SENDING: January 18, 2015

Dear FutureMe,

I am thankful for these things:

difficult challenges from which sometimes I learn something
a hobby that keeps me employed (computers)
arguing kids because I can then appreciate peace, quiet, and harmony
Internet
Book of Mormon
Scriptures
Savior Jesus Christ
12 step programs
taste buds
pizza
wife and nine kids
shelter
food
clothes
cars
innocence of children
atonement
the Holy Spirit
the Millenium

temples

sex

most of the world can speak the same language

sunshine

rain

VoIP phones

open source software

Linux

cell phones

Asterisk Open Source PBX

Ruby programming language

Python programming language

WRITTEN: January 02, 2006

SENT: January 02, 2007

Dear FutureMe,

i dont know how many times i have written futureme letters to myself
that are about sexuality and coming out, but i know it's a lot. but i havent
gotten any of them back yet. which i guess is a good thing because i
havent done anything and if i got all those hopeful and scared emails i
would just feel like more of a
coward than i already do.

i had a dream a week or two
ago that i went back in time
and i saw myself at the age
of ten. and i thought maybe
i would tell her that when

> **"I was totally dumbfounded
> that I had been told off by
> my younger self."**

72

she grows up she will realize that she likes girls and see what she said. but before i could even say anything, she knew what i was going to say and she turned her back. she wouldnt talk to me and then she got angry and told me i was being a coward, that i just get myself all upset and then use that as an excuse not to act. i was totally dumbfounded, that i had been told off by my younger self.

and i felt so ashamed.

so wherever you are when you get this, you better have come out and moved on with your life and dont you dare come back to haunt me in my dreams. cause i am going to take charge.

soon.
Love,
c

WRITTEN: March 22, 2006
SENT: March 22, 2007

Dear FutureMe,

random emails are fun :) I went to a strip club for the third time with g. yay! hahah i got my first ever lap dance. she seemed to be the only girl in the club that wasnt stoned out of her mind. she had a nice body, i dont know why but i cant stand large breasts or shaved pubes. when breasts are big and fake they seem odd, kind of like old chinese foot binding or lip disks or burmese elongated necks. and when theyre big and real they seem droopy even if the girls in her late teens or early twentys.

as for pubes i think its kind of wierd just because up close it looks prepubesant and ive tryd it once and it iches like crazy! My favorite part of a girl is her legs, i like it when a woman has shaply calf muscles i hate when you cant see and differance between the width of the ankle and the calf :-(

Im desperate for a girl right now i havent had a girlfreind in well over a year :-(I love g. and hes great in bed but some times i just need to feel another womans body agianst mine as her hair brushes against my neck as we kiss and i slip my hands under her clothing … *sigh* thats enough for now.

WRITTEN: January 08, 2006
SENT: January 08, 2007

Dear FutureMe,

You know what my worst fear is self?? To have never done anything … to have simply allowed myself to go through the days of my life finding no meaning in either my life or my days … Sad isn't it?? To think that's what happens to some people!

But I'm not sure about the meaning of MY life … No self, I am not thinking about offing myself. I might have my problems and stuff but certainly I'd never want to throw in the towel … Where was I??

Oh yeah, I've been thinking about maybe becoming a missionary … whaddya think??

You know another one of my worst fears??

Realizing I have lived an ordinary life!!

I don't want to live an ordinary life! I want to live an EXTRAORDINARY life … I want to go, do, touch, and smell and love and experience my life!

And I guess at this moment in time I feel a bit like life is passing me…like I'm sitting on the sidelines watching everyone else do what they want with their lives…I know it's probably terribly selfish…and it is but still, a girl has needs, doesn't she??

I think maybe, and this might sound crazy, self, that maybe just maybe Satan might be trying to make me feel down. I know it's crazy!! Especially since I've never been on his most wanted list…but I don't know…I've always thought that I MUST have a very big purpose to my life…Sometimes I think I can almost feel something in me shouting at me that yes! yes! There is going to be something HUGE about my life! Yes! I will touch other people's lives…I might suffer for it but I will…I'll make a difference…

I know, I know…alert! alert! There's a wacko in my head! But it's like the second time I've thought about it and well, usually if something is crazy or stupid I don't think about twice…I just think about it once and then it's gone but this thought seems to stick with me…

Also I haven't done my devotions either today so perhaps that's it too! Sigh…

Anyway, I gotta go!! Feeling very frustrated, mad, angry, upset, discouraged, overwhelmed, etc, etc!!!

Love,
Your Self—moron! LOL!

WRITTEN: February 03, 2006
SENT: June 16, 2006

> "I don't want to live an ordinary life! I want to live an EXTRAORDINARY life!"

Dear FutureMe,

Today is Friday, March 24, 2006. I am 23 years old. I'm by myself in the apartment which is very close to school. I am sophomore in Dental Hygiene program. I have a boyfriend and his name E. He is in the army right now. He was supposed to be discharged within two more months. I have a roommate, too. Her name is P. She is with her mom now. So I am completely lonely. I was just thinking about talking to you. Ten more years, I'll be you. What do you think that I will look like? Will I be pretty or rich?

Sometimes I'm scared of future. Will mom still be there with me? Dad passed away two years ago. I miss him very much. I was suffered a lot when I lost him. I'm afraid that one day, mom won't be there any more for me, you know. So if mom's there, would you tell her that I love her very much. And I wish her all the best. Wish that she can still be healthy and living with us.

> "Watch out for your husband. Do not give him freedom. If he has too much freedom, you'll lose him."

Are you married yet? Who is your husband? I wonder how he looks like. Is he handsome? Is he a good husband? Does he take care of you and love you and your family? I truly hope that he would be a good husband. And I am very curious who he would be. And how about you? You should be a dentist by now, right? How does it fell to you when you finished school? Do you feel like you just take off a big debt? But I bet you will have some new debt. Family, kids, husband … a lot of stress, right? But always remember to take care of yourself. Always keep yourself beautiful, that's a good way to survive in the world which has a so many jerks. Watch out for your husband. Do not give him freedom. If he has too much freedom, you'll lose him. Man ... they can never be trusted, remember. You are doing good in your business, don't you? I believe that you just graduated from dental school. I really truly hope that you graduated from dental school. Don't let me disappointed, please. Never ever quit. You are my hope. You will enter the age crisis now. At this time, you will have so many things happen in your life. Must be a lot of stress. But I have a faith in you. I know that you can do everything. Be strong.

How's N. doing? Wow, he should be 17 by now. Is he still be a good boy? Still in school? Hopefully. Does he get involved in any bad stuff? Teenager, you know. It is very hard to keep him now. Just hope that he's still be my little brother. How about T.? Is he married? Ugh ... remember the nasty girl that he loves? She was so cheap. She made me so mad by luring him away. You know what? She told P.'s parents that she'll go to Kansas for college homecoming. But you know what? It's all a lie. I bet everything that she's with your brother right now. Ugh ... cheap cheap cheap girl.

But most important, how about you, my dear? I love you so much, so so much ... I am thinkin about you, you know. You must very beautiful and elegant by now. If you graduated, mom and dad will be so proud of you. So proud of you. Do you miss them? Yeah, I miss them too. Do you meet a lot of cute guys in school? Are they hot? Yum ... I love hot guy, tall and pretty and brown hair ... they are so hot. Oh, one more thing, I would like to know about your boobies ... yeah .... your boobies ... Are they getting any larger? Need to take care of that too, ok. Never forget to keep yourself up. You are a young beautiful lady now. You take care, ok. I'll talk to you soon. I love you very much. Bye.

WRITTEN: March 24, 2006
SENDING: March 24, 2016

dear futureme,

stop talking to j. he's a jerk and he just makes you cranky. but being a jerk to him *does* make you laugh sometimes.

are you with k. yet? do something to make that boy not so shy goddammit. he's a good kid...i think...

are you all recovered from the cancer? i bet the scar is sweet as shit.

pack those bags for alaska, ms. n.!

k.

WRITTEN: March 28, 2006
SENT: April 28, 2006

Dear FutureMe,

So right about now you are probably freaking out about how to pay bills, make friends, and deal with living in a new place. My guess is also that you're going to be nervous as hell about making it as a writer. The last few months have been tough. But you're sending this email to yourself to remember that you've made it through tough things before, and you will make it through tough things again. Take walks, remember to live fear-less-ly, and take time to relax and comfort yourself. This is walking through the rain time, and the rain always stops or you find shelter in the storm. And remember to congratulate yourself on the things you *have* accomplished ...

go take photographs today. snap pictures. draw with crayons. make watercolors. learn spanish. visit a library. make friends with the neighbors. think outside the box to solve a problem.

Live in ways that are ruled by the love you give out, not the fear you feel.

WRITTEN: May 06, 2004
SENT: November 01, 2004

> **"Live in ways that are ruled by the love you give out, not the fear you feel."**

Dear FutureMe,

It's 1 in the afternoon, but your hip hurts so you mixed Hawiian Iced Tea and vodka. Your mIRC window is flashing and your fantasy role playing freinds think that you are lying down.

You are still scared about working in the Phone Sex industry despite your mother's blessings (assuming, of course, that your hands are busy making art to sell on eBay while you moan your way to a living) and you're currently peeved at some 15-year-old who goes by the handle 'C.' who thinks you're a Nazi, a drunk, and an all around evil no-good-nik. R. is also giving you a headache with her 'holier-than-thou' act, and you have a slight crush on T. despite never having met him in real life.

Why so obsessed with the online world? Because your Seattle life hardly exists. You invited K., the girl in #408, to go with you to the Arboretum but she already had plans to do the Underground Tour. Have you done either yet? Because you wanted to do both, but your hip hurt too much. Granted, when you sober up, you will think to yourself that your hip didn't actually hurt so much … but it does. Trust me. You blame yourself from being fired from Pemco because of your hip … because you missed so many days. It hurt. Honestly. It. Fucking. Hurt.

You also miss F. Terribly. Perhaps that's why you bonded with T. He yelled the nice and reassuring things at you that F. used to do. That you're worth something even if you're not being clever. That you're quite simply amazing. That your father is WRONG. What he did to you is WRONG. Naming you after that girl who he wanted to bang, but wouldn't have anything to do with him because she was being raped by her father? WRONG-WRONG-WRONG-WRONG-WRONG. And Shameful! SHAME. Shame transcends "wrongness" to you somehow. It digs deeper. You can do bad things and still be a good person. You cannot be a good person with shame.

You have captured the hearts of … well … dozens. Not millions. Maaaaayyyybe a couple hundred. There are a great deal of people infatuated with you, and you view yourself as some kind of Muse—inspiring many but ultimately feeling that she has been denied her own person who is worth creating art over. Do you love yourself? Yeah. Alot. Sometimes. And then you hate yourself. Alot.

You're also terribly lonely. You try to visualise the perfect man in an effort to make him manifest before you, much in the tradition of the inspirational tapes that you heard during milk runs with Aunt N., but it doesn't work if you don't get out of the house it doesn't work. Men don't come to your door like pizza does. You need to get out. Even if it's just for coffee.

You're also still bitter about your father. Is the fucker dead yet? He's had cancer forever. And he's still an ass, Christ forgiven him and all. Still. An. Ass. You called your mother for comfort and all he wanted to know was if you needed money. You did. He sent you $200 via PayPal ... the equivalent of a nice tip for him ... which means that in a way he cares about you ... but in another way he didn't ask anything to your face about ANYTHING. You only heard his voice on the other line yelling "Does she need money again???" Does this betray love, or does it betray that he sees you as a burden for whom he can 'save'?

And yes. I'm still drunk.

Have you succeeded in having an out-of-body experience yet? Yesterday, you had something awfully close. And you tasted blood in your mouth. E. let you hold her for what seemed like ages while you scared yourself silly, licking your finger to see if blood was actually there. But E. was a good sport. She's a good kitty.

You still keeping in touch with D., L.'s brother? He loves you too. That's a person who would take a bullet for you. And he's sat with you for maybe a total of 48 hours? You're just that intoxicating.

"You have captured the hearts of ... well ... dozens. Not millions. Maaaayyyybe a couple hundred."

Speaking of intoxicating, you happen to be the victim of vodka right now. The glass is empty and you feel like singing a sad and slow Jason Webley ballad right now.

Remember in Canada where you practically walked on muddy water while your norse freinds got their hems muddy?

That's what you do, M. You walk on muddy water. It would seem like a miracle, aside from the fact that you did hours of research to get to that point. But it seemed fun at the time, so you didn't notice the work involved. But to everyone else? Baby, you seem like a supernatural phenomenon.

They've told you so.

Remember me,
M.

WRITTEN: January 21, 2006
SENT: January 21, 2007

Hi there from your past self. Weird to think that you used to be me, but I don't exist anymore hey? I'm essentially dead! But don't be sad 'cause if I wasn't, you wouldn't be here would you?

> "I hope you have things a little more figured out, because right now I'm lost on what I really want..."

I hope you have things a little more figured out, because right now I'm lost on what I really want and that is bad 'cause then you have to just take what you get 'cause I didn't do anything for you! I'm sorry for that.

And now that you know how it feels, maybe you can get some things going for Your future self!

Good luck, remember how awesome you are because you are me but even better 'cause of course, you know more than me, and are probably hotter 'cause you have more money so you can buy lots of clothes and stuff…

Good luck with getting through the worst part of winter, when Christmas is over and all there is to look forward to is Valentine's day and Easter before summertime.

From Me

(Remember? you'd just gone to that banquet the night before and gotten that call from M., hah.)

WRITTEN: November 07, 2005
SENT: January 09, 2006

Dear FutureMe,

You should be getting this on your 50th birthday, if I did our math right—we never were good at math. Remember how sad you were about forty? Remember the night terrors and being that achy sadness all the time (gee I hope that stops soon). Well now your fifty and I bet you feel really stupid about being so upset about forty. It's like when we were in school and spent all of 6th grade wishing we were back in 5th and never enjoyed 6th … same with 7th wishing we were back in 6th … and on and on.

You always have had a habit of wishing for the past, being scared of the future, and not enjoying now … STOP IT!!!! Enjoy being 50. It's not so bad really ... is it? Your thinner than you were at 40, at least you better be. If you're not you could have been. So get on that.

And hey at least there isn't a baby screaming and kids fighting as you read, cause there sure is while I'm writing. Oh who am I kidding there probably is, hell the twins are only 10 now, T., C. and L. are 13. At least I hope they are, the twins are sick now.

Wouldn't that suck if they didn't make it, now I would have gone and made you cry thinking about them. Now I'm afraid to ask you any-thing ... Oh my god what if S. isn't here anymore. I sup-pose me bringing him up couldn't make it any worse than it already is. I can't even imagine how you must feel if he's not there. If he is you better go give him a big kiss right now!!! I hope your here to read this.

> **"You always have had a habit of wishing for the past, being scared of the future, and not enjoying now ... STOP IT!!!"**

Now I'm thinking this is really dumb. What could 40 year old me pos-sibly have to say to 50 year old me. I'm sure 50 year old me would have plenty to say to 40 year old me. I wish you could do that ... now THAT would be good. What can I tell you that you don't know? Hmmm. maybe that's it though. Maybe somehow you are telling me now.

I'm telling you feel good about 50, to stop looking back, stop being scared—enjoy today, to do something about your weight if makes you so fucking sad. But you know really, your telling me the same thing (as I sit here crying eating doritos). You can tell me buck up and enjoy the moments because the big things are gonna happen no matter what, and being so scared about it only takes all the joy out of life. I hope I can figure out how to do that, because I'm having a real hard time right now.

I do see I'm the only one who has the power to make life good for you, my 50 year old self. I hope I didn't let you down. If I did don't hate me too much, I did the best I could, I really did.

I pass it on to you now. It's up to you to make things right for the 60 year old us … (And you know she wants to hit the road with S. in a Winnebago and never look back. You better start saving cause she's gonna be pissed if you don't get it for her. LOL)

Now stop crying … oh cause I know you are … big sap … and go do something for your birthday, I bet the family will be here soon.

Have a blast, and have a drink to me.

ME

WRITTEN: January 13, 2006
SENDING: November 27, 2015

Dear FutureMe,

In June of '05 all you could think about was "I'm fucked". I'm living outta my car (which cannot go backwards), the best advice I get for the movie biz is to be someone's bitch as an assistant ("but look at all the successful people who were assistants" [or drivers or ___]), I haven't been laid in a decade and it's the second most thing I think about. Thinking God is going to come outta heaven or wherever He resides to give me a hand is unthinkable (and thinking that way makes me think that He won't give me a hand all the more just for thinking that way—a classic catch-22).

So how did you do? If you're living with your mom in OR you may as well pimp yourself out to some midget porn site cuz it ain't goin' on. Or, did you focus on God's graces and make some headway in entertainment? Maybe even got married (K., are you still out there?)!

M.

PS: Don't go to Mexico without lots and lots of bottled water. AND, don't drink ice tea down there—what do you think the tea is made from?

WRITTEN: June 04, 2005
SENDING: June 04, 2010

Dear FutureMe,

I can't seem to decide whether or not life is good. I have a good job, a loving wife, a new house, a new car. It seems I'm living the dream. But sometimes I don't feel it. I feel like I'm meant for something, but don't know what it is. And of course don't have the time to figure it out.

I hope by now maybe you've figured it out. What is it? If you haven't yet, then maybe sit down and do it.

So much can change in one year, so I imagine a ton has changed in 10 years. Who's died? Who's been born? What happened to all our friends?

Remember you can be crazy, and life is better when you let yourself have fun. Fun the way you want to have it. Be yourself, and never be sorry for it.

Love ya.

WRITTEN: November 07, 2005
SENDING: November 07, 2015

I've never been in love. This is an awful thing, because the truth is, it makes me feel like a child. Professionally, I am not a child. I am very capable. But personally, I have no experiences. I have never successfully dated. I've never been kissed. I am a virgin; this is a choice, this is intentional, but I work with people who not only are not virgins but can't imagine *being* a virgin. Without knowing my specific choice, without thinking about it, they ridicule virginity. They all have dated, they all have been in and out of love, and I have not. I feel trapped. Somehow I can't cross the line into adulthood. I cannot have a relationship.

I do not drink. I do not smoke. I do not take drugs, and I do not drink anything with caffeine. I never have. I tell myself this is because the body is sacred, although the truth is, it's a hard decision for me to maintain sometimes. If I ever did drink and lost my inhibitions a little bit, I think I would become addicted to the sensation. I try so hard to loosen my grip on my total control over

"Without knowing my specific choice, without thinking about it, they ridicule virginity."

myself and the situations I'm in, but I can't. I don't seem to know how. I often think that what I want more than anything else is a guy who can force me to lose control and still be safe. I love to be blindfolded. I love to be told that I'm going to a certain party or something whether I like it or not. I love to be picked up, especially without warning. I love anything that says, "You're no longer in control." Maybe I get tired of being in control.

I believe there is a plan for people. My heart tells me so, and I have had experiences that make me feel stage management is a definite part of my plan. What scares me, though, is that I've never had an experience that makes me feel marriage and children are part of my plan. I want these things DESPERATELY, but I've never had the feeling that makes me sure those things are going to happen for me. I can only hope so.

One of the things I want more than anything else is consistent people in my life—friends, or even better, one consistent person—a husband. I even have a "wedding ring"—a gold band that I think came off of a button. I wear it occasionally on my left finger, when I am alone. I'm wearing it now. It's silly, ridiculous, something a very young child would do, but I do it anyway, I think because it's a symbol of everything I want so badly and am terrified may never happen. It makes me feel protected. I have friends I know from college, and I still keep in regular touch with K., T., M., E., J., S., T., and R., but these are people I may very well never see again, and I certainly don't see them on any sort of regular basis. I hurt for companionship.

My biggest wish? That five years from now I'll say, "How silly I was to worry so much about all those things." My biggest fear? That five years from now I'll say, "And nothing has changed."

Fear thou not.

E.

WRITTEN: December 25, 2005
SENDING: January 01, 2011

Yesterday I found out about you … I never felt so many feelings and emotions crash on me all at once until I was told I was going to be a mother.

I was told all my options/abortion/adoption … or just being your mother like I'm supposed to.

I could never take your chance to live life away from you. So abortion was completely out of the question …

But I don't know if I am ready to give you my life in whole … If I decide to raise you myself … I am robbing not only myself, but you as well … to have the life I want you to have and right now I don't know if I can give you that life … I know that your father would do anything for me and you to be happy forever … but I'm only 19!!! … I have always been told that God would never give me anything I couldn't handle … I never knew it would be right now??

And I want to apologize ahead of time for all the problems you will face when you are older … I am sorry for doing drugs when I knew

"I am robbing not only myself, but you as well …"

I was pregnant but just didn't want to admit it to myself … Im sorry for the addiction Im sure you will have … to whatever … I dont know … but its so unavoidable in my family … I will help you with it though … to avoid it as much as possible and to just be a good person in life … no matter what I decide I will love you more than you will ever know … you havent even taken a human form yet I have a love so unbelievable just for you only … that I don't know what I can possibly do with it until the day I see you … so to my baby … I love you more than life itself more than my life … more than any boy I ever thought I loved and I love you more than I can even put into words … they tell me I should expect to see you sometime around the 21 of April 2005 … so I will write to you again to keep you up to date.

WRITTEN: September 14, 2004

SENT: April 21, 2005

I'm so sorry for all the pain and confusion you will experience in your life one day … and I feel solely responsible for it.

Today I called the adoption agency. I know I told everyone that I was going to keep you and raise you to be the amazing person that I know you are going to be … but I just can't. I'll never be able to give you all the things that you will need or want in life … I can't even do that for myself … I cannot even tolerate your birth father anymore …

I will be moving out of his apartment shortly … I am planning on moving in with A. in a tiny little 500 sq ft apartment in Vista, CA … But I find that to be highly unlikely … only because I don't know how good she is at paying rent and bills … she claims shes fine with bills, etc … we will see …

I was for a quick second thinking about having an abortion … but I can never do that … I saw your tiny little heart beat not more then 3 weeks ago and I could've just died right there …

Everyone is telling me that I'm not going to be able to give you up once I see you but I know that if I didn't I would be breaking alot more hearts than mine … I promise you, my baby, I am going to find you amazing parents that will raise you and love you better then I can even imagine … they will send me pictures of you and letters telling me about all the amazing things you are and will accomplish someday …

I can only hope and pray that you understand and realize that I am doing this out of love. I don't want you to hate me for what I am doing … I can only hope your future parents will raise you to be an understanding and forgiving person and that someday we will meet and you will see all the love I have been saving for you your whole life …

WRITTEN: October 09, 2004

SENT: May 21, 2005

90

on this date, march 12th, 2006, i was in love and loved by d. we have just moved into an apartment together and he is sitting behind me on his computer. we do that alot—face in opposite directions. when we sleep. when we're awake. sometimes, i get lonely like that but i'm learning to adapt.

i think i am too emotionally high maintainence.

WRITTEN: March 12, 2006
SENT: March 12, 2007

365 days

Dear FutureMe,

This is just a reminder that it was technically your year (06) to have the kids on the 4th, but because you let your ex manipulate you, he ended up with the kids on your year. No need to go into all the drama about this, just know that you were not happy about how it worked out. (Although you did end up watching the fireworks with T., which was an unexpected delight to the evening.)

So when you read this, on July 2, 2007, its to let you know that yes, 07 is technically your ex's year, which he will undoubtedly tell you, but... don't forget, he had them in 06—so consider this a notice of the switch.

And hey, keep smiling. Even though all this divorce crap sucks, at least you're not married to him anymore!

From your past self...

WRITTEN: July 05, 2006
SENT: July 02, 2007

Dear FutureMe,

You're in college now! Or at least, I hope you are. Is your roommate an asshole? Are you friends with him? Are you completely apathetic towards him? Does he think you're weird? Does he think you're gay? Does he know you're gay? Is HE gay? Have you hooked up with him?

WRITTEN: March 07, 2006
SENT: October 02, 2006

209 days

dear me,

how's life treating you? for me, its going ok ... been out of the hospital
for a week now ... we had viral meningitis, which is the better of the
2 meningitis' ...

the family is good ... dad found out last week he has to stay on chemo till
november ... it made mom cry ... but at least he has the anti-depression
drug, its helping keeping him sane, and therefore keeping us sane ... R.
comes home in june, and i'm scared to death of him leaving again, as it
means he'll be on his way to iraq ... marines have it hardest of all and the
way R. is, he'll want to be front and center for everything ... i'm so proud
of him but so terribly scared at the same time ... you and the parents
haven't talked about it, cause it makes you all cry, but stop reading this
again and go write him a letter ... and draw him a pic, you know how he
loves our stick figures ...

B. is over in iraq right now ... its hard as hell ... he's your best friend and
its hard not getting to talk to him face to face ... has he been home or did
he go to australia with the bitch?

remember also that i love you with all my heart ... no matter who you
turn out to be ... just do your best and leave the rest up to fate ... life
is good ... and it will all be ok in the end ... if its not ok, its not the
end ... stick to your guns, stick up for the little people, stick by your loved
ones ... and take some chances for the love of pete ... you won't get anywhere if you don't ... leap and the net will appear ok ... i love you

WRITTEN: May 17, 2006
SENT: November 20, 2006

93

Dear FutureMe,

well. it's been more than a month since i worked. save more money if you're freelancing, stop paying for everyone when you go out, and stop blowing so much on getting drunk. for health, if nothing else.

i am still smoking. if you are as well, quit, you dumbass. for health, if nothing else.

i just called A., my real mother. we had a 45-minute conversation, a few days after the three-year anniversary of Mom's passing. remember the 15-805 junction at 9 pm that night? anyway, talking to A. was a little weird, if you don't remember. i'm still not quite sure what the point is of re-opening this can of worms. no, i know what the point is—it's to try and get over trust issues i have in my life. what i'm not sure of is how to get there. what do i say to her? do i want an apology, a more detailed explanation ... what? the irony is that the trust i can't give others is because of her, and now it's hampering my ability to talk to her ... it's come full circle. about 10 minutes in, i felt like i wasn't really talking to her. it felt like an old neighbor i felt obligated to talk to, because i was asking about her husband, the new house, the new job, the vacation to Europe. i could give a shit. i mean, i want to, but i don't know how. i think i need to bring up the old stuff, the bad stuff again, air it out. i may invite her to LA this week. we'll see how it turns out.

the other reason i wanted to write you again is that i'm still thinking about D. a lot. almost every day, if not every day. shit, it's been over two years, i guess, but i still think about her. i think about how cruel i was, about how quickly i can let a good thing go and not care about someone else's feelings. about how hard it is to trust. about how easily i can let someone else's opinion affect my decisions about a good thing in my life. about how tense i was about how my father might perceive her. i mean, there were other things that were affecting my emotional state at the time, namely my mom's death and being so far from what i wanted in my career. but right now, it's been three years since mom's death and i'm much closer to seeing my career blossom. and i still think about her. L. and i were drunk the other night, and he asked me about her for some reason, and i talked incessantly for thirty minutes about how i screwed up and how frequently she visits my mind. then, the next night, she drove by me on 6th street in the blue Volvo. what a trip. i wondered if she saw me. i wonder if she thinks of me whenever she sees a silver Prelude? she turned into the parking lot for Cafe Bleu, so maybe she still works there … anyway, L. and i agreed that unless i am certain my feelings for her are true, that i should keep my trap shut and not try to speak to her. it wouldn't be fair to her for me to utter any words that aren't a thousand percent pure and true. i would much rather live with my uncertainty than hurt her again.

> "It wouldn't be fair to her for me to utter any words that aren't a thousand percent pure and true. I would much rather live with my uncertainty than hurt her again."

so, chin up. and do some of those while you're at it. take your vitamins. no more m. night shyamalan movies, unless maybe it's someone else's script. keep trying to write.

good luck.

WRITTEN: July 24, 2006
SENT: October 24, 2006

Dear FutureMe,

Why are you so lazy? You have to finish your college applications. It's much more important than organizing files on your computer. That's all you've been doing today and jacking off. If you had NOT masturbated from past weeks, you could have used the saved time to write a goddam novel, you stupid. The family is in bed and you're about to watch porn aren't you? Aren't you???? Right?? You fool. Face your fear and get started. Remember the hardest part is taking the initiative. Begin. Go! Wait Family Guy is on in 5 minutes, lemme watch that first.

WRITTEN: January 29, 2006
SENT: March 29, 2006

---

hey babe

grow up.
and if you are grownup, growdown.
nobody likes a wretchedly old person.

WRITTEN: March 16, 2006
SENDING: February 23, 2013

2536 days

Hey man,

This is the 13 year old you.
happy birthday.
Did you get your business degree?
harvard?
princeton?
lake washington technical?
Well on my end I am work-
ing hard to get in E.'s pants.
Did I?
are you cooped up in some
bank, writing fucking re-
ports for 60k a year?
Go.
go see the world. pass out
in india.
wake up in africa.
smoke weed with buddhists.
LIVE
I know you though
you wont go
your a pussy
but I want you to go.
I need you to go. buy plane tickets right now.
Rise with the sun player.

Kisses,
L.

WRITTEN: January 29, 2006
SENDING: August 07, 2022

"Go see the world.
Pass out in India.
Wake up in Africa."

Dear FutureMe,

OK. A. . . . awww . . . we get along soooooo well. the butterflies in the stomach. the sickening endless texts and emails. argh. i want him bad. but. he's engaged. we havent done anything yet but i know we will. and i know im gonna fall. i have a feeling he will too. i am making it my mission to make that happen lol. i've done it before. but only when i have thought there was potential. and that was once. with S. if he gets married i don't think it would last. or if it did it wouldn't be a happy marriage. A. would never stop fucking around on her. i know it's crazy but i can't help this. and if he doesn't fall? WELL . . . i guess that could happen. doesn't matter. i'll just enjoy the journey and deal with the outcome when it gets here.

by the time i re-read this . . . i wonder if i have him yet. i give it 6 months.

WRITTEN: February 06, 2006
SENT: June 07, 2006

Dear FutureMe,

Was it worth it? Are you still with the man who left his wife for you? Were all the tears worth it? Or, has he done to you what he did to his wife? Only time can tell whether all the tears, pain and anguish were worth it all. I hope as you are reading this (or should I say, as I am reading this), that you are still together and the story has a happy ending.

"Remember, there are no bad decisions. The best decision is the one you made at the time."

98

In reading this e-mail, you should remember all the steps that happened to you to get here (whether it worked out or not). Lots of lessons were learned along the way and lots of pain was experienced by many people, not just you. Always remember that no matter what the outcome.

Remember, there are no bad decisions. The best decision is the one you made at the time.

PastMe

WRITTEN: December 19, 2005
SENDING: December 31, 2010

Dear FutureMe,

I am sitting here crying thinking of how to get out. Do I still love him? I don't know. We are two people who really should not be together. Growing up together made the transition so easy. He was always my friend so why not take it further. He had always loved me but I was always unsure maybe I should have listened to that voice form the beginning. I just wanted to be loved. He was always the one who was always there. He was the one who always loved me no matter how unlovable I was. However just because you grow up with a person does not mean you will grow with them.

We are so different in every way. It is good to have differences but this is too much. We are not the same people we were when we fell in love and we are growing further apart every day. He has different values beliefs and passions then me and can not even respect me for who I am. He yells at me calls me names and still expects me to take care of him and give him scratchies. He needs me more then he loves me.

There are times I am determined to make it work and feel I love him so much I can not breathe without him. And then there are times like now where I inch towards the door dreaming of walking out. Not too long ago I stratled the railing on our 22nd floor balcony swaying back and forth feeling the breeze and the freedom I could bring to myself. I thought that if I could not walk out the door and leave I would jump and leave everything. But of course too many people depend on me and I would feel too guilty (even though I would be dead) to leave them all so selfishly.

He always makes me feel guilty and bad about my self. So I won't give him a blow job why is that so important and why can he not respect my feelings? I can see him cheating on me because of it and maybe I hope I catch him so I can have that push to walk out.

What am I doing? I am married to this man that makes me feel awful about myself and scared for the future. He needs me more then he loves me and we are both afraid of life apart that we suffer through this existence.

When I get this where will I be? Will things be wonderful and I'll be wondering what was I thinking? Or will this become the extra push I will need to leave if I am not already gone?

WRITTEN: January 02, 2006
SENDING: January 01, 2008

Dear FutureMe,

Today I write to myself on my 30th birthday. I'm currently 24 years old with every aspect of my life together, except my relationships. I have two serious boyfriends. I really don't know how this happened, but I have two serious boyfriends, both of whom are in love with me. On top of this I have one other person who I have been seeing on and off for two years, who I am in love with.

"I really don't know how this happened, but I have two serious boyfriends…"

I hope that by the time I have turned 30, I have grown up and met someone I am able to love enough to marry. Right now, it seems as though whenever I meet someone great, who treats me the way I would like, I push them away. Case in point—my two serious boyfriends who would walk through fire for me.

Not many people know that I have two boyfriends, other than my family and closest friends, but it is difficult! I travel for work so I am only home on the weekends and I have to juggle my time between the two of them. Sometimes I wish that I would get caught and this charade will finally end, but I never have and I wonder if it ever will. I care about them both in different ways. One was my college sweetheart, who is about to finish law school to become an attorney, and the other is a writer in the entertainment industry, with great dreams and the means to attain them. My college sweetheart is my age and the second is about to turn 30.

Dear Self—I am writing you in hopes that by the time I have turned 30, I have waded through all of my commitment issues and learned to love just one person. In truth, I'm not that hopeful. I haven't changed much in the past 4 years.

Oh well, when it doubt, choose the one with more money!

WRITTEN: March 28, 2006
SENDING: September 10, 2011

Dear FutureMe,

When you wrote this e-mail, you just knew this local girl for less than 1 week yet you are falling in love with her beauty and innocence. She is the Perfect girl for you; she is beautiful, intelligent, tall ... everything. You have been in this god damn place for more than 7 months but WHY DID YOU ONLY MEET HER NOW??? WHY??? I mean why not 6 months ago? Why not even a month ago? Now you are going back in about 10 days and what at first seems like a dreadfully long day has turned into a speeding bullet. I DONT WANT TO GO BACK!!

But how bout your responsibilities back home? How bout all your commitments back home? HOW ABOUT YOUR FAMILY BACK HOME??? I am soo confused now. You are thinking of extending my work here indefinitely for this girl you just knew for less than 1 week. Is that stupid of you? Or is it taking the chance ...

You have about a week to clear this out ... What to do? Please TELL ME!??? ... WHAT DID YOU DO???

WRITTEN: March 30, 2006
SENT: April 30, 2006

"... you will be the Eric B. & Rakim of dads."

Dear FutureMe,

I know you sweat and every muscle in your body gets tense when you have to hold a baby, but when M. is born you will be the Eric B. & Rakim of dads. Stay strong. Babys are hard to break. For god sakes, they spend 9+ months in a womb, in positions that Yoga Masters are uncomfortable with. Then they come shooting out of a 9 cm opening, and manage to keep it together. When you read this, you will be a pro and have an amazing daughter.

Love,
Me

WRITTEN: January 22, 2006
SENT: April 30, 2006

Dear FutureMe,

Today is a joyous day. Your beautiful sweet baby was born one year ago today, 11 weeks early.

On this day last year when you went by her isolette to catch a glimpse of her, on your way from the surgery recovery room to your regular room, all you saw was this little precious bundle weighing just 2.1 lbs.

> **"And you felt like this tiny being barely larger than your hand had just reached out and taken your heart and claimed it for herself."**

And you felt like this tiny being barely larger than your hand had just reached out and taken your heart and claimed it for herself. It was the most heart warming and horrifying experience all at once. And the only thing that kept you going was looking up at her daddy, your wonderful supportive husband, and seeing the tender smile on his face that reassured you that everything was going to be o.k.

Months later, when we knew she would be fine, he would admit to faking it just for your sake.

And what an incredible joyous year it's been. You are the mother of a healthy, beautiful, sweet child that brings more joy and beauty into your life than you ever thought possible.

I must remind myself to make sure I thank my baby for all the good love, for all her wonderful smiles, for all her giggles that are wonderful music to my ears.

WRITTEN: January 10, 2006
SENT: April 10, 2006

Dear FutureMe,

i hate you.

but on a lighter note, i hope you have started studying and have made decent progress …

i'm not gonna go off on you anymore because a) it's 1 am, and b) i want to have a wank.

but i hope you aren't a failure.

WRITTEN: October 02, 2005
SENT: January 01, 2006

91 days

Dear FutureMe,

I've certainly accomplished a lot in the past year. Since just last August, I've:

—taken a couple courses, which catapulted me onto the sex party scene.

—gotten engaged, while dressed as Santa.

—been promoted twice.

—got an article in Playgirl magazine.

—landed a lunch meeting with an editor at Women's Health.

—appeared in a Women's Health article.

—bought a condo.

My goals for the next year:

—be promoted at least once more, or else find a cool mag job.

—be published in Women's Health, Marie Claire, and more!

—become a master networker.

Just think… two years ago, I had been unemployed for quite some time, and was just beginning my internship at the Feminist Press.

WRITTEN: August 17, 2006
SENDING: August 17, 2008

Dear FutureMe,

Wherever and whatever you may be, I hope that you are genuinely happy. When you go to bed you actually want to wake up the next morning and spring into action. Though I doubt you've stumbled across the meaning of life, I believe that you've accepted your limitations and recognized the full scope of your abilities. You know your likes and dislikes and are not afraid to voice them as the case may be.

If none of the above is true, and if you are still the sniveling creature that I am now, cowering in the shadows and wracked by bouts of rage and depression, I hope you put an end to your misery. Sell all your possessions and go out into the world. Find religion. Rent a car and take an indeterminate break. Yes, it'll be scary, but remember that a sense of uncertainty, even fear, means that you just

> "Life is risk. Deal with it. Or just kill yourself. I bet that painless technology to do that is already around."

might be on the right track. Life is risk. Deal with it. Or just kill yourself. I bet that painless technology to do that is already around. Donate your organs to individuals who really want to live so that your existence might not have been entirely without meaning.

Tomorrow I'm taking the FSWE. It is totally off my supposed track in life, but what the hell. It might force me to open up to new experiences. And that's one thing you need—coercion and an organized plan. Stop resisting order and linearity. What are you so afraid of?

Love,
PastMe

WRITTEN: April 22, 2005
SENDING: April 22, 2010

Dear FutureMe,

Got your letter yesterday. Thanks a bunch for the stock tips!

WRITTEN: March 28, 2004
SENT: March 28, 2005

---

well well well future me, its past you! how awesome are things in the bright shining light that is 2015? flying cars? robots? toasters that can talk??!! remember when you had jobs that you didn't really like and thought you'd have a cool one by now? did that happen? past you sure hopes so. remember when Google was just a search engine and didn't rule all of North America and Eurasia with an iron fist? remember mp3's, how much better are mp64's? Remember shows about previous decades? how was "I love the 2000's"?
remember intelligent design, what was up with that? oh wait, you found out alien overlords actually created us? Scientologist aliens? using magic? wow, i did not see that one coming, good luck with all that. in conclu-

> **"Remember when Google was just a search engine and didn't rule all of North America?"**

sion, I hope you are not lame, future me, drop me a line some time if you want to go for a drink (but i guess you'll have to wait till time machines are invented and since we haven't met up yet, i suppose you're waiting for just the right time).

WRITTEN: November 07, 2005
SENDING: August 28, 2015

Dearest FutureMe,

So! Have I moved by now? Mom and Dad said I could have a dog when I move. Do you have one yet? (You'd better have one, man. They promised. Show them this e-mail if they deny it!) What kind do you have? Right now I like beagles. I also like pugs, but they snort.

See ya,
M. (*Now*)

P.S. Are my ears still big? :-)

WRITTEN: July 20, 2006
SENT: September 20, 2007

Dear FutureMe,

Happy Birthday Me! How are things in the future? As for here in the present things were going alright until today, which leads to the next question … Have they discovered how to send emails back in time yet? If so, please, please, please do me a favor and send me an email like 3 days ago (2/12/06) and tell me NOT to set the laptop case upright on the desk with the LCD side facing the power converter and mouse. It will crack the LCD when it falls over and that will just suck considering the repair cost and the fact that we haven't even had it a week now! Also, I'll send you a list later of women that you should warn me about! :) Hopefully, this finds us well and past emailing is available (and affordable) in your time, I suppose I'll find out once I press send …

WRITTEN: February 15, 2006
SENDING: October 27, 2027

Dear FutureMe,

Writing to my future self is kind of strange because I always hope that I will have improved. As of this writing, I am rather in a rut, which I recognize. I've never been a particularly happy person, so it is probably vain to hope that I would be one year from now. But if you're still basically in the same place I am, you should try doing all those things that you're always putting off, like exercising and getting your shit in order.

This would be a lot more useful if it worked the other way around. I would be a lot more inclined to follow advice from a future than a past self, since my past self would basically just be me minus a year of experience.

> **"I would be a lot more in-clined to follow advice from a future than a past self..."**

So maybe (hopefully) you've got it all figured out in the future, but I sure as hell know my past self didn't know what the hell he was talking about. Which is probably the situation you're in now.

WRITTEN: February 16, 2006
SENT: February 16, 2007

Dear FutureMe,

Send someone a love letter anonymously. Someone lonely, sad, and depressed. Much like yourself in this moment past.

WRITTEN: December 20, 2005
SENT: February 05, 2006

Dear FutureMe,

Hey. So today might be a sad day or it could be happy. Who knows what's going to happen with dad. PLEASE just make sure that you take extra-special care of mom today. (Like I even have to remind you.) If dad is still around, just think about what a miracle it is; if he's not, then try to keep it as normal as possible. Whatever that means.

> "If dad is still around, think about what a miracle it is; if he's not, then try to keep it as normal as possible."

Right now I'm feeling like dad will hang on for a little while and somehow I can see him there at Christmas time. At least I sure hope so. Never know, maybe that miracle will happen.

OMG … I just remembered … DO NOT FORGET ABOUT THE CHRISTMAS CARD THAT DAD WROTE FOR MOM!!!!!!!!!!!!!! Now where did I put it. I'm going to put it away right now and then tell you (me?!) where I put it … Hang on …

Okay, it didn't fit in my green jewelry box, that would have been my first choice. It's on the dresser behind my perfume bottles. Big white envelope.

Now, maybe you should think about not giving mom the card while people are around. Think end of the evening … Unless dad is still here—then give it to him to give to her himself. Now wouldn't that be a special gift??

Well, try to enjoy your day, remember, it's your favourite day of the year.

WRITTEN: September 23, 2005
SENT: December 25, 2005

110

Dear FutureMe,

Hey now is it really you? Oh my God it is! See I told you you could do it! You got through the chemo and you kicked cancer's ass! So what if you're bald, that just means more variety in hair styles and color. Hey, go buy yourself a punk rock wig ... just for making it. You are my hero, self, you really are!

WRITTEN: May 21, 2006
SENT: October 18, 2007

Dear FutureMe,

Okay, so one year ago you stumbled across this website and decided you'd have a little fun. Here's the plan. Every year, once a year, when you've received one of these, you must send out another one that same day, to be mailed in one year from that exact date. Each time one is written, make sure you include all the highlights of your life. Make sure you save them, too! Lord knows we're horrible at keeping journals. Maybe this will help?

2/28/06

Amazing things in my life:

I'm a Second year Junior at university

I'm in love with C. We broke up on January 3rd, but just this past week I convinced him it was a good idea for us to get back together. Yay for not giving up!

I am learning Mandarin Chinese. Do I still know any by the time I'm getting this?

Mom and T. are still together and are taking a trip to the Panama Canal.

I "dated" my high school Econ teacher, M., for about one week, doing everything, before realizing he could never be C. So I ended it.

I work in the Education and Psychology Library on campus.

On October 28, 2005, your suitemate and friend killed herself by jumping in front of a train.

WRITTEN: February 28, 2006
SENT: February 28, 2007

Dear FutureMe,

So are you still who I am? Or have you changed yet?

Maybe you still need a cold one, you Type-A neurotic freak.

Oh, yeah, I said I wasn't going to do that. Kinda depressing when you see everyone else slamming their future selves for the things that they haven't improved but definitely should have. I suppose I should just keep swinging. We always want to be better. But negativity is just counterproductive. So don't stay where you are, you aren't anywhere close to perfect. But don't revile who you are now, you must crawl before you walk.

It has been my experience that folks who have no vices have very few virtues. —Abraham Lincoln

Lata,

-z.

WRITTEN: October 06, 2003
SENT: April 06, 2004

> **"But don't revile who you are now, you must crawl before you walk."**

Dear FutureMe,

Happy 21st. You're probably going to get drunk to celebrate, aren't you? Good girl. See, back in 2006 when you wrote this, you were about to turn 18 and had never had a sip of alcohol in your life.

You're probably going out with friends or having a party of some sort, at least. You couldn't do that for your 18th birthday, because you had no friends. You secretly wished for a surprise party, but knew nobody would ever throw one for you.

In fact, you were quite pathetic. Earlier in the year, you tried to kill yourself because your Australian boyfriend was going back home. You failed (obviously), just as you seemed to fail at everything then. You were a third year freshman, damn it, you needed help. Your depression and social anxiety were taking over your life, and you would starve for days on end because you were too afraid to go out in public to get food. You wouldn't do assignments because you were afraid of people reading your writing. You would skip class if you thought you were going to be late because you believed people would make fun of you for it. Your parents knew nothing about any of it.

I'm telling you all of this in the hopes that you now see it as a completely foreign way of life. With any luck, you have gotten over these issues and you're a completely different person now. You were very, very unhappy that way. (And if you are still living like that, you need to do something drastic about it. Now.)

I don't know where you are now, or whom you've become. I don't know if you've found love, happiness, or even somewhere to live. All I can tell you is that when you wrote this, you had none of these and it wasn't working out well for you. Remember the way you were, appreciate how you've grown, and continue to work towards improving your life … you need it, and you deserve it.

Love,
PastMe

WRITTEN: September 07, 2006
SENDING: November 06, 2009

Dear FutureMe,

Right now I am bent. I just weighed myself and I weigh the same damn amount I did last week, 204 lbs. My percent body fat is 23. I am 7 weeks into the second body for life 12 week challenge and am frustrated with the lack of progress. I started at 214 lbs, 10 lbs in 7 weeks sucks ass. I should be at -14 lbs. What the Hell is wrong with my body fat, it should be lower. If it is not 22 next week, I am going to break that scale as a public service.

I feel like I sacrifice 6 days a week. I bust my ass on a treadmill 2 times a week to the point that I think I might pass out, pedal to a near heart attack on a stationary bike that feels like it is buried in sand, and push like I'm the first man to give birth lifting the same stupid dumbells or weighted pullys. I am trying to improve my physique all the while surrounded by natural beauties who simply get a gym membership to flaunt their God given perfect asses around in tight spandex.

I drink 2 goddamn protien shakes a day, eat potatoes with salsa, salmon and chicken, and don't forget the fucking cottage cheese and yogurt (never get tired of that shit).

I eat this health food while I smell the delicious greasy burger breath of my coworkers, or, even better, get food chunks shed on me as they eat candy bars or other forbidden items right in front of me.

When will I look like the 'after' picture? When will this diet become easy? Seems like some weeks are hard and others are not. Sometimes it takes every last bit of willpower within my very soul to resist the neverending buffet of free

> **"But I hold on to the hope that one day I might look in the mirror and see something attractive."**

food that is all but shoved down my throat at work. Brickoven pizza, bagels, candy, popcorn, soda, and "Hey everyone, lets go do lunch at the best tasting restaurant in Dumps-ville, USA, my treat." My voice cracks when I say no. My resolve is so paper thin sometimes, just one little excuse and I could take a swandive into a steamtray of greasy ribs slathered in barbeque sauce.

But I hold on to the hope that one day I might look in the mirror and see something attractive. I hold on to the hope that when I read this again, I could reminisce about the time I almost gave up; I almost did. But for a simple, stubborn, angry, insane and sick and tired of the same shit collection of reasons I don't really know how to describe, I will go on; even if every week a scale says 204 lbs and 23 percent bodyfat, I will continue. I am changing everything my life was based upon as I continue my personal quest to find a way out of this labrynth of fat I have built around my body.

Hope the person that reads this knows how important he is to me.

WRITTEN: November 21, 2003

SENT: November 21, 2004

Tomorrow is the first day of the rest of your life. People always say that, but for us obese people, surgery day really is the first day. Don't worry about a thing, it will all be ok. Dr. M. is a great surgeon. Hope you're having fun eating sugar free jello and broth. That looks like life for the next couple of weeks. Aren't you glad the bowel prep is over?? Gross. Well, remember that I love you, and everyone is pulling for you to make it through the surgery with flying colors. Good luck?

(ps: If the surgery date has changed, then go to FutureMe.org and send a new letter to yourself for the new day before surgery. I hope that you don't have to do that, though.)

WRITTEN: March 18, 2006

SENT: April 18, 2006

Dear Me,

Please tell me you've aged gracefully and haven't done anything stupid … like cosmetic surgery.

So the girls may have needed some lifting, ok. So the furrow between your brows from many concentrated study sessions and years of staring at a computer screen may have needed to be, how do you say?, ironed out, ok. So those 15-odd gray hairs multiplied faster than a calculator, ok.

But it doesn't matter, sweets. You're still hot.

WRITTEN: January 16, 2006
SENDING: May 17, 2010

1582 days

> ## "I understand that you're either a robot or dead by now. I hope you're a robot."

Dear FutureMe,

I understand that you're either a robot or dead by now. I hope you're a robot.

How's life? I probably didn't set you up to be very successful but I trust in your resourcefulness. If you didn't do anything particularly interesting or rewarding in the last 20 years I'm not mad. You are a robot after all ... I imagine your days consist of conforming to your alien master's every desire. Hopefully those desires are cool and they send you on outrageous adventures to distant galaxies.

I love you,

A.

P.S. WB if there's a www.PastMe.org.

WRITTEN: February 14, 2006
SENDING: February 14, 2026

Dear FutureMe,

Humans are weird. We make terms up for things we shouldn't be able to understand. God probably laughs when people are in physics class struggling with the idea of gravity. I just took my Physics final today and we had to use a formula to calculate the force of gravity at different distances from the earth. A number called something like the gravitational coefficient, a number in the formula no matter how far away you are from the earth, was like 6.64x10 to the 24th N(m) to the 2nd x ... I mean seriously! How do we know that kind of stuff! I'm sure it's pretty accurate, but my feeble brain does not comprehend how we can invent science and figure out crap that shouldn't even concern us. I don't think humans were meant to be in space, or put things in space like satellites to help us watch tv and spy on people in Moscow. I bet God invented gravity real fast.

There I go again. How do I know God invented anything. Everything is a piece of him. I didn't invent my kidneys just because they are there. The Bible just says he spoke and everything was. Geez, writing about all this really makes me feel like humans are silly. Or maybe it is just me.

I just read a book by this guy about how he spent a month living in the woods with a bunch of hippies who smoked a lot of pot and drank too much beer. He noted though how they loved each other, and himself in a more genuine way, than he had ever encountered at church, an institution he had grown up in his whole life. I started thinking about how I have been subconsciously judging people since I popped out of the womb.

"I have been subconsciously judging people since I popped out of the womb."

I don't know why I am the way I am, but there are many things that I think are bad, and if I encounter them I have an overwhelming sense that I have to get away from them. One of them is smoking.

When I was growing up, not like I'm done or anything, but when I was younger my parents always let me know if I was doing something bad and told me never to do it again. They formed in my head a very guilty conscience. Or maybe it's a feeling that I must be obedient. Either way I have always had a sense of right and wrong that led me away from everything wrong. Well, not everything but most things. This I have discovered in recent days has been an impediment to my ability to love as well as forming the thought that I am a better person for staying away from everything bad. The biggest thing though is my ability to love. When I see people doing "bad things" my head says, "stay away, that's bad." I know it sounds stupid, and those words don't really go through my head, but the notion that people who do bad things are bad people is a horribly wrong assumption.

Back to the smoking idea. Yes it is bad for your health and carries an unpleasant smell, but if when I walk down the street and see someone smoking and the first thing that pops into my head is "stay away," how am I ever going to bring Christ to the world? Why would people listen to me when I say Christ has brought me more love than I have ever known if my snobby aura in life says nothing but I'm better than you because I have found JESUS?!?!?!?

As I was reading the book, I realized what a snobby jerk I must have been seen as while at school telling people not to cuss, and half heartedly asking people why they haven't been in church, yet all the while proclaiming my faith. I can definitely see why people do not want to go to church or even approach the idea of Christian love. It is because of people like me.

The day I read the chapter on love I made a decision that I wasn't going to be me anymore. I needed to be Christ to everyone. He was not afraid of people that looked like they might be carrying a gun or be plotting an attempt to rape him. OK, those are things that I am afraid of, but really, he loved everyone. Hard to understand, but he did. Even when he was dying on the cross, he asked God to forgive the Roman soldiers who nailed him to the cross. That night I had a meeting for a mission trip to Costa Rica and on the way in to the church there were like twenty people outside of it smoking and looking kind of conspicuous. The me of a couple hours prior may have just put my face to the ground and hoped they didn't say anything rude while my ears were still in listening distance, but because of my decision to love, I smiled and said good evening. That doesn't sound like much, but they almost looked surprised that I would even acknowledge them and wish them a good evening and yet thankful that I did. It felt freeing to see how they responded and accepted my gesture.

I am still new in my outlook of love, but I pray that I will not lose the ability to love. I am finding new aspects of people everyday.

When you simply love people, they are a lot more tolerable.

It used to be that a lot of people annoyed me. People that would say things that no one really wanted to know or people that wouldn't shut up no matter how many times you thought you made it obvious that you didn't want to talk. But when I realized that everybody needed love and that that was more important in the eternal scope of things than me being comfortable and me spending time with only the kinds of people that were just like me, it

> **"When you love people, they are a lot more tolerable."**

opened my eyes to the beauty of life. There were endless relationships that I could pursue with people, not because I thought they needed me to love them, but because I actually wanted to love them. I am sure that if you are genuine in your relations with everyone, and truly love them with patience, kindness, gentleness and all the other fruits of the spirit, that they will be much more open to the ideas of Christ's love than any kind of bible thumping strategies. It is through relationships that people receive the love of Christ. Without receiving love from humans, how can we know what God's love is like?

WRITTEN: January 13, 2006
SENDING: May 26, 2008

I suppose I could be contemplative about writing to the FutureMe but, really, there's only one thing I need to know: Did I get laid?

I hope so.
xo, me

WRITTEN: December 20, 2005
SENT: July 03, 2006

Dear FutureMe,

Sorry! I take full responsibility for your wretched life. I just dicked around the internet for all of 2005 and 2006 instead of pursuing relationships and skydiving and whatever.

WRITTEN: May 22, 2006
SENT: May 22, 2007

365 days

Dear FutureMe,

you're a lesbian and you need to accept that.

you're not sinning you're not wrong. the only wrong thing you've done is
hide it like something to be ashamed of.

tell people.
i'm giving you 3 days to tell people.
now, i'm in the past so i can't actually hurt you or anything.
but just know that if you don't you will be letting your seventeen-year-old
self down.

remember the gap commercial with that sexy girl on it?
remember your crush on the girl in your art class senior year?
remember reading gay fanfiction?
remember viewing female porn accidently? and then staying on the page?
remember right before you wrote this wanting to tell mom?
remember how good it felt to tell n. and a. and k. you were bisexual?

think of how good it will feel to be open about being gay.
admit it to yourself.
admit it to the world.
you'll like yourself more.

WRITTEN: March 20, 2006
SENT: May 09, 2007

> **"Admit it to yourself.
> Admit it to the world."**

What are you like? This whole "writing letters to your future self" plan
is so nice, but I wish I could get a letter back from you, or write one to a
past self. I would do it all the time.

123

"Dear self from last week,

Don't yell at her for not eating the whole thing. It's not her fault—she has a disorder & she needs help. She's not doing it to piss you off. Calm down and talk to her about it, get her an appointment with an anorexia/bulimia specialist. You can do this. There's no need to be mean to her."

"Dear self from 4th grade,

Yes, it's sad that S. wants an abortion, but think of the way J. treats her. Maybe it would be her best option. Stop judging her so harshly and think for a second about what you might have to do in her situation. Understand that the world is not always black and white, and that sometimes we all need to do a few not-so-great things to deal with the gray areas."

"Dear self from 9th grade,

Don't go near G. He's only going to hurt you. Find some people you really like and stop just seeing people because it's convenient. Have some self-esteem. I promise things are gonna get SO much better! Just wait for summer and you'll see what I mean."

Yeah, those all would've helped. But maybe this'll help you when you get it. I hope you're doing well, coping with college alright, and not beating yourself up too badly or stressing out too much. You're still beautiful & smart & I hope you've figured that out.

Much love,
The Old You

WRITTEN: June 17, 2004
SENT: June 17, 2005

Dear FutureMe,

You are home on leave with the woman of your dreams. Make love to her often, take her shopping, laugh, enjoy her company. In a few days you will have to go back to that shit hole Iraq and it will be another three months before you can hold her again. Savor every second with her.

WRITTEN: March 20, 2006
SENT: June 01, 2006

Dear FutureMe,

If you're still working in Iraq, get the hell out of there. 21 months is way too long. Go home and drink a beer.

WRITTEN: July 05, 2006
SENT: June 05, 2007

World War Three. When did it start? When did you know it started?

The world is slowly starting to realize that the Israeli defensive strikes against Hezbollah a week ago, and the ensuing violence in Lebanon, was probably the beginning of the third world war. Or perhaps Armageddon, in which case you'll never read this anyway.

Is this morbid? Maybe so. I don't really think so though.

I look forward to Christ's return. I hope the would-be prophets are right when they say the signs are here. I hope this is the end.

I cry tears of joy thinking of the day I will finally be reunited with all those who have gone on before. Do I dare hope?

WRITTEN: July 19, 2006
SENT: August 18, 2006

Remember that boys are dumb. This will help when you are freaking out about the current boy in your life who is taking his sweet time while you wait around for him.

WRITTEN: June 10, 2004
SENT: June 16, 2004

Dear FutureMe,

today you have one year off drugs and off alcohol. a year before this you were smoking crack, could not shower or bathe, was drinking a half gallon of vodka every 24 hours, couldnt get a job, just quit stripping, was dating an abusive man in the army, was lonely, wanted to die, only had 4 friends and they were crackheads, had no relationship with your parents, hated everyone, wanted people to give a shit about you, hit a school bus drunk at 3 in the after noon

the you that is writing this is ten months sober and confused about life. but the obsession and craving to do drugs and alcohol is gone. you are happy, joyous and free. you live with mom and dad and are in school, doing really really well. you work at a full time job that values what you do for the company. your car is gone but dad lets you drive his new minicooper when you need to. you eat and shower and brush your teeth every day. you are a fully participating member of the recovery fellowship you belong to. you have a Higher Power in your life. you have people that love you. you are useful. you are content. you have a life you did not think possible.

how can this be something you did yourself?

A Power Greater Than You is Working in Your Life.

i love you.

that is an odd thing for me to say about you today. but it is true.

WRITTEN: September 01, 2006
SENT: October 27, 2006

> **"The you that is writing this is ten months sober and confused about life. But the obsession and craving to do drugs and alcohol is gone."**

Dear Me,

It's been a little over a day since he passed away.

Please don't forget him.

But don't dwell on the past. It happened for a reason. God has a plan for everyone and in this case, his plan was for him to save fifty other lives. I guess that makes him a hero of sorts. Even in death, he's making other peoples' lives better.

There's nothing that could have been done to stop this. There are such sick, twisted people out there and it's a shame it had to happen to such a good kid. So just remember the good times and don't forget what a great person he is.

Sincerely,
You

WRITTEN: March 25, 2006

SENT: April 25, 2006

Dear S.,

Here's a story I want to tell you, in case you've grown a little complacent, or your eyes have gotten a little cloudy. Still getting to the gym at least 3 days per week? Still running at least 10 miles per week? Well good for you, if you are. But hear this story, and let it really resonate with you, regardless of how you're doing. It might be helpful.

One day, while finishing some chores tonight before bed, I suddenly flashed on Oprah's "make the connection" videotape, which I had watched years ago. I flashed on that moment when she talked through clenched jaw and teary eyes about how much time she felt she had wasted. Wasted. That she'd never get it back, any of it. I thought about my own "wasted" time—wasted years of being young and cute and carefree, when dating was easy and fun. Why had it taken so long to "get it"? And I realized, it's hard because it's not a pretty thing to face, and frankly, food's more fun. It's hard to face every day just what you're doing to yourself, what you've done to yourself. And oddly enough, food helps to hide from that reality. It's a lovely little escape, those little morsels, where you feel so good for the moment that you can pretend you're ok. Pretend you don't have a problem with food. Pretend you're just like everyone else. But you're not just like everybody else—this is the monkey that will always be on your back. And when you stop and take stock of exactly who you are, without food there to help you hide from that, then it gets hard.

So make it your goal to make sure every day is a little hard. That way, you'll know you're still awake.

If you're not doing so well, that's ok. Just open your eyes. Everything begins with awareness. It's ok. It's hard, and it's every day. That's what life is about.

WRITTEN: March 27, 2006
SENT: January 06, 2007

129

Dear FutureMe,

i cant believe i did that. the warehouse bathroom??!!

WRITTEN: February 16, 2006
SENT: November 14, 2007

Dear FutureMe,

Today marks a month since I sat upright in bed at 5am and wrote C. a final letter. It's been a month and two days since I found the love letter and learned the truth; that she was having an affair. It's been nearly two months since the last weekend we spent together—a weekend that I now know was filled with lies. Our four-year anniversary, no less.

It's been the worst, worst winter on record. My days have been lonely and sad and long and terrifying. Sometimes I feel like I'm going to die from the grief and pain. I've never, ever suffered this sort of trauma before. All at once, I love her (was in love with her, am falling out of love with her), miss her terribly, and hate her, I HATE her for manipulating me and deceiving me and cheating on me and falling out of love with me. And treating me so badly it takes my breath away.

In my strong moments, I can feel myself getting better. I can see that the space she and all of these emotions occupies in my body and soul is getting minutely smaller each day. I can feel that happiness and strength and healing are creeping in and filling that space. I have moments where I can envision a happy life without her. In the space of a month, I found a new apartment, moved in, found new friends, started running and losing weight, got a promotion, and am creating a life independent of that relationship. And going on a date with a sassy lawyer tonight. I surprise myself every day!

And in my weak moments, the movie reel takes over and I'm paralyzed by remembering the letter, by imagining her with L., imagining her lying to me. No one has ever treated me so badly, and I can't stop my imagination from running wild. It's so awful—and I berate myself for doing it to myself—and end up miserable.

All I can do during these bad moments is try to get through them. All I can do is check out, tell myself to breathe, feel the pain and just grimly put one foot in front of the other. During the next month, I want to keep seeing friends and making new friends, I want to successfully run a 5K and keep training for a 10K. I want to think about going on a few more dates. I want to get

> **"All I can do is check out, tell myself to breathe, feel the pain and just grimly put one foot in front of the other."**

plenty of sleep, and decorate my new apartment, and cry a little bit more than I have this month to let out some of this grief. I want the space she occupies to grow ever smaller, but I also want to forgive myself if it doesn't happen as quickly as I want it to.

I want to have good days and bad days. I want to walk home with a smile on my face. I want to laugh and enjoy spring in NYC like I never have before. I want to excel at my job. I don't want to initiate or have contact with C. And maybe, just maybe, I want to have sex.

I want to heal. We'll see how I do.

WRITTEN: April 13, 2006
SENT: April 13, 2007

Dear FutureMe,

Hey, happy birthday.

Did you get into med school? I will have to kill you if you bollocks'ed up the interview. You cocky shit.

Hope you havent slept with L. Hope you have slept with C.

Cheers,
Me

WRITTEN: July 15, 2006
SENT: December 29, 2006

Dear FutureMe,

Remember how fucked you were that night?
And you genuinely felt this liberated you from him, in a sense.
You stuck those fifteen needles in your chest
(That's thirty total holes—entry and exit)
As you listened to his favorite CD
All the while thinking of him, no?

Don't deny that
And you listened to that CD a second time
As you removed those fifteen needles
And masturbated to his music and the sweet release of those needles leaving your skin

But not to the memory of him

(Come to think of it … he never did once get you off, did he?)

And then as the CD ended

And you were left with thirty bleeding holes in your chest

You took that sweater he gave you

(He put it on you right after he asked you to dance naked in the rain with him that night, before you went to the cafe together)

And you bled all over that sweater

It's your favorite

WRITTEN: April 20, 2006

SENT: June 20, 2006

Dear D.,

I'm typing up something that I wrote a while ago, but didn't finish until now. Speaking of which, my first advice to you is: stop procrastinating! That is probably your greatest impediment against your success. You know as well as I do that self-control and self-discipline have always been difficult for you to master. Keep in mind that the small things add up. Get to school on time, brush your teeth at least 6 times per week, don't fart in school, stop staring at girls, don't breathe so loud (or with your mouth open), and most importantly, speak with confidence.

So, guess what was on your mind back then? Here's the first sentence of the first draft: "I hope you're not still a virgin!" But now I don't really care that much, as

"…brush your teeth at least six times per week, don't fart in school, stop staring at girls, don't breathe so loud…"

long as: 1) your weird obsessions with certain girls stop, 2) you control your porn addiction (waste of time, if you ask me), and 3) you are comfortable with females. You can't be comfortable with a chick if you're constantly thinking of fucking her, so don't be a pervert. And remember, there's someone out there for you.

Be an intense person. Running can be a pain in the ass, but it is also great for learning, thinking, and transcending routine existence. Same with tennis, and all sports. There may not be a God, but I'll do OK as long as I can sweat my heart out on a tennis court.

Are you still libertarian? Whatever your political views are, you had better still be outspoken about them!

More may come later. If not, this has been fun, and I wish you the best of luck for the future.

Your friend,
D.

WRITTEN: June 06, 2006
SENT: March 01, 2007

Hello.

This e-mail is a reminder of a bet made on Sunday May 14th 2006. Bet states that V., by this time (May 14, 2007), will be obsessed with a girl who he'll think is the one. Her name will not be L. Obsession constitutes this girl not liking V., and him still sticking around because she's the one.

WRITTEN: May 14, 2006
SENT: May 14, 2007

Dear me,

hello there. So yeah right now, life is so great. I have great friends, that im gonna tell you about. I have an awesome boyfriend. And i get everything i want.

The only bad thing about life right now is school, and my grades. I have 4 f's 2 d's 2 b's and 1 a-. But yeah its cause im stupid lol.

N e way about my friends, they are so great. First there is r., Hes hott and awesome. Then d. M., I havnt hung with him in a long time, but he is a dur dur. Then a., shes kinda like me in a way, like all dark n sinister. Then there are the preps, d. T., and s. D. is the poser. Then theres c., I went out with this moron for about 5 months lol, we broke up about 5 times, but i still love him as a friend.

I have a new boyfriend right now, and he is the greatest thing that has ever happened to me. Im so in love with him, he is always callin me beautiful and he is so great. His only flaws: he doesnt let me drink or smoke and he doesnt let me cut myself, but yeah. He is so great. Hes my sister t.'s best friends brother. And his name is m. Any way about the rest of my friends. There is the ghetto group who is m. aka muffin, n. aka five, and w., then theres j. And b. whos nicknames are t and box/cookie lol. My nicknames are gir and turtle and yeah well i cant think of anything else to say, but i need to bring up my grades and get rid of my drinking problem!!

"I need to bring up my grades and get rid of my drinking problem!!"

WRITTEN: April 08, 2006
SENT: August 15, 2006

Dear FutureMe,

You laughed for the first time in two months today. Congratulations! The object of your amusement was a four year old girl continuously banging her head against a window for no apparent reason. You nearly had a hysterical laughing fit in public watching a child kill its brain cells. You sick fuck. I sincerely hope you've found something better to laugh at by now.

WRITTEN: February 10, 2006

SENT: June 26, 2006

R. . . . you have been married for exactly one month today . . . you love him so very much yet for some reason you notice a light hint of doubt mixed with guilt . . . last nite you saw W. . . . it was a nice visit . . . it helped create some closure with everything between you and him . . . you now know you can go on with your life not feeling bad anymore . . . you also talked to M. . . . after talking to him you also felt a great big weight had been removed . . . R. you have done so much with your life since him … you would have never been where you are today if you had to continue on with him … you love him but not because you want to but because you cant let go of everything when it comes to him … but you once again got some closure from talking to him and feel much better with the choices you made … however now the main event is about to commence … D. called this morning wanting to make dinner plans with you … he doesnt know that you are married … why havent you told him?? you know why but dont want to admit it which is exactly why you have feelings of doubt and guilt with you husband … D. was supposed to be the one "to save you" … do you remember the last 3 years? … he saw you in all your fading glory of drugs, crime, and self inflicting pain … and he still loved you … or maybe thats what you thought however you still kept holding on to the dream of maybe someday he will want to marry you … but now life has a strange way of directing you of where you are truly meant to be … so now here you are … sitting in front of a computer screen in So Cali … 10 am drinking a beer waiting for that

> "… and all you want to do is figure out the meaning of not life, but just your own and where it will take you …"

fucking Seargent to call you into work … and all you want to do is figure out the meaning of not life, but just your own and where it will take you … you are secretly hoping that D. will be upset that you are married and tell you that he made a mistake with you and wants to make things right … but you will still stick to the vows you made and tell him its to late … and secretly hate it … maybe you should cancel the dinner plans and just go the bar with A. … but you wont … hopefully you wont drink yourself into stupor and embarass yourself like you did at the last dinner

you had with D. … remember you love your husband … hes a good
man and doesnt deserve you being a dumb bitch … just go have dinner
get some closure once again … and move on with your life … and go
home to your husband in a week … love him like youve never loved him
before … he deserves that

WRITTEN: July 21, 2006
SENT: July 21, 2007

Dear FutureMe,

The baby is due in two days and we are really excited.

Hope you are still doing good, and baby and S. too.

Did we get a shotgun yet?

WRITTEN: October 24, 2005
SENT: October 24, 2006

Dear FutureMe,

I hope you still dislike marriage and kids. If you've fallen head over heels for a guy, then please re-think it! Marriage is nothing but trouble. He will steal your money and leave you with a big headache! And kids are money-sucking, whining animals. But I don't think your opinions on kids will have changed much over the years. At least I HOPE not. LOL.

WRITTEN: August 10, 2006
SENDING: August 10, 2011

Dear FutureMe,

youre 18 as you write this and have never been kissed, except for in abuse.

the year you get this you will be turning 25.

if you have yet to recieve a kiss from joy or love or 2 sided lust, then i want you to take 6 aspril. it won't kill you. but maybe it will shock you into stop being so afraid.

WRITTEN: May 15, 2006
SENDING: January 19, 2013

Dear FutureMe,

first i thot i'll send u this message in the year 2008 but ur 23 ur turning 24 in july.
Of course u'll be married end of 2007, i.e. 19.5 months.

did you have a love marriage?

"Did you have a love marriage?"

i don't mean to make you feel bad if you had an arrange one. but i just wanna let you know to stop feeling bad about it. and if you had a love marriage hehe (may be god blessed u with love and u say "lol" like him and no more hehe) does your name, your first name and his last name, roll of your tongue and how is your signature looking after all the practicing that you might have done … i dont know how u ever became so amazing that in 19 months u went from being friends to husband-wife. cause the current me cannot even imagine the struggles you'll face/faced, you will have to take classes to cook non-veg. food or have diff. culture kids with him. remember ur sister-in-law's nightmare (u should explicitly give him details if he's next to you reading this).

if you have an arrange marriage think about positives in life—same values and culture, same economic background, u don't have to keep working—working could actually be a sport like many of ur married friend's, that u take on to keep urself entertained and let the other women in your kitty-parties know how corporate you are. even though you will be leaving your father's house nothing will really change.

just remember what ever u do be passionate. things will work out and u never know, ur sweet husband might actually be the man u totally fall for, if and only if u give him a few chances.

in the end try to forget what u couldn't have and move on. he makes u laugh so what, u can come up w/better jokes to share with ur hubby. remember nothing wrong w/ dreaming just don't expect them to come true.

hope i didn't confuse u or make u cry.

WRITTEN: May 18, 2006
SENT: December 31, 2007

All people posting public letters on this site ask themselves if they've followed their resolutions: if they've exercised, stuck to their diets, whatever they still hadn't done when they wrote the letter. Alternately, they incessantly ask questions that can't possibly be answered.

As of April 11th, 2006, my life is pretty good. I'm not organized enough, and I don't budget my time properly. I probably won't in 2007 either, but there's always some hope. As of this instant, I'm putting off a Graph Theory assignment due 16 hours ago, and hoping I can also finish a Database Systems project and still study some for Organic Chemistry.

I love N., dearly and desperately. I agonize over the thought that we really won't work out—I've known it from the beginning, and I hope to hell it all goes as well as it might seem to. If it doesn't, I'd like to remind you how wonderful she was, and how good she was for you. No matter what, it was worth it. I hope (and feel confident) that you loved her as much and that no matter what, you were also good for her.

> "I agonize over the thought that we really won't work out—I've known it from the beginning ..."

You don't have to be getting a second degree, you don't have to be getting a graduate degree. I hope you will, but it's really a childhood fantasy that only might have real use. If you're as stressed this morning as I am a year ago, take your mind off it a little and think about how good your life has been, and all of what's ahead of you. Actually, go ahead and do that anyway.

WRITTEN: April 11, 2006
SENT: April 30, 2007

Dear FutureMe,

It's a little hard starting this letter, knowing that three years from now I'm going to be reading it and seeing it as quaint or niave. My words, which I say in earnest now, will cause me to cringe and the seriousness of my past self. I will undoubtedly chuckle at how I once articulated my thoughts and thought about my life. I will find gramatical errors and spelling mistakes and other slippages that only time and perspective reveal. So future self, have sympathy, look kindly, you were once a past-self to another's future.

S. left about an hour ago. She was tearing up a little bit as she got in her cab. In the past few weeks there's been moments when I found myself looking forward to saying goodbye. In this relationship, I sometimes feel stifled and a little constrained. Sometimes I think we have different priorities, different tastes even. I've even thought that I couldn't marry S. But I love her. I love her. I worry that I don't let her know enough. I care about her. I was looking at pictures on the Facebook and found one of her. It caught me off guard I felt a little tinge of something. I look forward to her visit in July. I worry about the limitations of phone conversations. I look forward to the way things might be next year, and I want us to come back to campus with the same amount of affection we feel now. Mostly, I feel that being in a relationship is complicated. There are so many aspects of my own personality that I have to get over and understand. But, in the rare, serene moments in my mind I find myself knowing, unquestionably, that I love her without complication.

In terms of the Future (note the capital F), I know few things with certainty:

-I want to help better the world however I can. Even if that process is a battle against unconquerable forces.

142

-I want to be creative in the way I think and in the way I act. I want to create. I want art in my life.

-I want to maintain my relationships. I want to maintain connections with the people who have passed through my existence.

There's probably other things. I'm in a sedated, kind of serious mood right now, it's gray outside and I'm a little tired. So this is all kind of serious. If I was feeling a little bit more bouncy, I might make quirky predictions that you could enjoy in their accuracy or incorrectness. I guess I just worry that you will be more or less the same as I am now. This is a question I've been pondering lately. Does our identity or personality ever fundamentally change? Are we the same unaltered base for our whole lives? If I was a better existentialist, I'd understand that I choose to be the way I am. Personality is merely a construct to give existence an essence.

> "If I was a better existentialist, I'd understand that I choose to be the way I am. Personality is merely a construct to give existence an essence."

Anyways, sometimes I think the personality I have now is the personality I'll always have. Which isn't such a bad thing, he's really not such a bad guy ... a little annoying sometimes. I'm tempted to give you advice to always allow yourself to be a little annoying sometimes. But that seems a little tacky.

The truth is I'm feeling exhausted. Thinking about the past and the future at the same time is a little trying. The most important thing is that I am well. I look hopefully to the things you might be doing soon. May this long, rambling letter find you well.

Your Friend,
Past Self

WRITTEN: June 14, 2006
SENDING: June 14, 2009

> "Note that you were too much of a coward to tell your friends and family the truth about your dismissal."

Dear FutureMe,

I am writing in regards to our offer of employment with _____. Due to your use of profanity and inappropriate responses in your application for security clearance, please be advised that our offer is withdrawn effective today, August 24, 2006. Please re-read the offer letter where we promised to pay you $60,000/year, and do not contact us again.

Sincerely,
Manager
Human Resources

PS: Note that you were too much of a coward to tell your friends and family the truth about your dismissal.

WRITTEN: August 26, 2006
SENT: August 26, 2007

Dear FutureMe,

I think you are currently in the midst of a transition. Just a few years ago, you shopped at thrift stores, and considered yourself an artist.

Now you are seriously considering going to business school.

So what are you now? Are you a sellout? Or was the younger me just naive?

WRITTEN: October 17, 2003
SENDING: October 17, 2008

1827 days

Dear FutureMe,

Fuck man, I don't know what to do. I'm almost positive H. wants to sleep with, or at least fool around with me, and I'm not sure how I feel about that.

I love J. I want to spend the rest of my life with her. I don't want to hurt her. In fact, that's the last thing I would want to do. I really mean that. I really would never want to hurt her.

But free pussy is sooooo appealing. Monogamy is stupid. It doesn't make any sense. If we were supposed to be monogamous people, we wouldn't have these feelings. Most birds are monogamous. They don't cheat since it's not in their nature to cheat.

For humans, it is not in our nature to be monogamous. So why do we do it? Society tells us to. It's a mechanism to prevent the few privileged beautiful men from keeping all of the women to themselves. Maybe.

Monogamy has its advantages. I have a deep meaningful relationship with my wife, one that I could never have with another person. If there is such a thing as a soul mate, J. is mine.

> "Monogamy is stupid. It doesn't make any sense. If we were supposed to be monogamous people, we wouldn't have these feelings."

But the closeness we have has NOTHING to do with sex. I love our sex life, it's AWESOME!!!!! She's fun and exciting and active, we laugh in bed together.

But there's something about free pussy…

H. would be a crazy lay. At the very least, she'd be different. I'm not looking for a long term mistress, and she's not looking to be my long term mistress, it's just something fun till we both get out of this shitty town, and go back to our homes, once this job is done.

Do I chance J. finding out? Will I ever be happy if I spurn H.? Will I always wonder? Or will it kill me with guilt if I do? This frickin sucks…

Future me, I'm hoping you're reading this and saying "thank God I chose to _____." If you're doing the opposite, try and take some solace in the fact that you put a lot of thought into it.

Peace

WRITTEN: September 13, 2005
SENT: September 13, 2006

Dear FutureMe,

It is a beautiful sunny winter afternoon in Perth. You have just been for a walk around Hyde Park and to pick up some minced beef from T.

You are 9 weeks and 1 day pregnant and you have been feeling a lot of doubts and anxieties, including:

Will i ever have fun again?
Will i ever feel carefree again?
Will i die of agony during childbirth?
How will we survive on D.'s income?
Will i finish my second book?
Will i ever write a third book?
Will i suffer from post-natal depression?
Am i a terrible person to feel all these negative things about being pregnant when i feel like i should be happy?

Of course you wanted to have a baby but it turned out you just couldn't imagine how you would actually feel about being pregnant until it happened and only then would all the dramatic changes and sacrifices you would have to make come to light.

So now your baby is one year old, hopefully. I hope you're feeling better about motherhood now. I hope your labour wasn't as long or as painful as you imagined. I hope you have a beautiful healthy baby and you love being a mum. I hope you and D. have come through all this difficult time and are still strong and in love.

I think when it comes to the crunch you'll be fine. Maybe you won't get there as quickly as some other people do. But you'll get there in the end.

Love,
PastMe xx

WRITTEN: June 16, 2006
SENDING: January 18, 2008

Dear FutureMe,

I desperately hope that when you read this, John Kerry will be the president. Or that you'll be working on moving to Australia or some-where. But I'd really prefer the first one.

Nervously,
You

WRITTEN: October 26, 2004
SENT: October 26, 2005

> **"I desperately hope that when you read this, John Kerry will be the president."**

Dear FutureMe,

If you're not a Granny yet, badger your kids. If you are, remember—it's not YOU who has to deal with over-tired, over-sugared and over excited kids. Revenge is sweet, so make the most of it!

WRITTEN: June 18, 2006
SENDING: October 18, 2025

7062 days

Dear FutureMe,

Hopefully your rich and famous by now and aren't one of those weird underage hippie parents.

In case your wondering what I was thinking when I wrote this... World of Warcraft servers are down and I'm about as bored as I possibly could be.

Peaceoutizzle

WRITTEN: April 26, 2005
SENT: July 20, 2007

Dear Fatty,

I can't believe you have this same email—only because it seems ludicrous to have such a silly email at this age. Today was a funny day, I hope you remember. You asked mum to buy a magazine for you on her way back from work—Cosmo, Vogue, wateva—you weren't fussy—it was stupid to ask your mother who has never bought one of those magazines in her life and has no idea where they're even positioned in a newsagency. So, instead she ended up buying you a porn mag without even realising what it was—(she just grabbed nething and paid and walked out) she said she saw a girl on it and just bought it assuming it was a fashion mag.

If she had read the cover I think she would've caught on:

*Jazz girl goes pubic with the public

*Lesbian on lesbian milk or something

*Why big tits ease the pain

I think you were so exasperated that you nearly cried. Then you found the humour of it all. Then you found it even more worrysome that she thought you should read it and enjoy? it anyway—then when you refused to have a look at it, she said dad should read it … I think a part of you died that day. lol …

Just a reminder why you love your mum and family—why no-one exasperates you, enrages and makes you laugh as much as they do—if anyone knows how to push your buttons too hard—it's them.

So get off your fat ass and do what you really have to do.

WRITTEN: May 14, 2005
SENT: May 14, 2006

150

Right now your plans are to attend law school in 2007, but before then … before you commit to a life of utility instead of passion, you are going to try to write a novel, your first, and you are already in the preliminary stages of research and development. I wish you the best of luck; perhaps writing won't turn out to be your bliss, but it will be better than sitting around wondering if it is.

Remember, don't ever settle—don't let guys persuade just because they want something and you want friendship. You managed to say no twice in a row now—keep it up! You deserve better than just being sexy. Make someone fall in love with you for your brain; it's the only thing about you that won't droop with age.

> **"Before you commit to a life of utility instead of passion, you are going to try to write a novel…"**

Stay gold, be confident, and find something to do that expresses you. The rest will work itself out. Trust me.

WRITTEN: May 22, 2006
SENT: May 21, 2007

I've been in school a long time. Going straight from undergraduate to a masters and now working on a PhD! What was I thinking? (wish I could e-mail past-self and ask …) So much research, so much time spent in front of a computer (a lot of it surfing silly, pointless websites), so many late hours in the lab. My advisor says I should finish in just over a year from now. Can't imagine that's possible! There is so much left to do.

So my question, dear future-self, is: did you make it? Were you really able to put together something "original" and "groundbreaking"? Were you able to get good results, and publish lots of papers, and impress people in your field? And tell me what happened once you graduated … I certainly hope you got some good job offers. That much schooling hopefully made that brain of yours worth something. Shucks, after living poor for all these years, you better be making the big money now.

Well, if you made it or if you didn't, I hope most of all that you are happy. Hope you remember to do things for yourself, things that make you enjoy life. Hope you have all your friends, 'cause those are most important. Hope you have your health, and dignity, and morals all still intact. And heck, hope you have a girlfriend too, one who appreciates you for all that you are.

Good luck with your future. I'll be sure to work hard to shape the next few years into something that is good for you, and you can look back on and smile at all the memories.

WRITTEN: April 11, 2005
SENDING: April 11, 2009

Dear FutureMe,

Your past me is at a crossroads. The Phd is done, but appears to have been a (quarter million dollar and 14+ year) waste of time. I hope that I am wrong and that later events will show that everything was good and necessary. B. will be five in May and I'll be 41 in a couple of weeks. Everything is beginning to bloom and I've planted ferns from Gramma—we just visited her to celebrate in our small way her 88th birthday.

I'm looking at this tome that took up so much of my life—and looking at the lack of teaching positions, the chances for me to get a job here that will allow me to pay back most of my debt before I die and feeling as though I should have gone to law school. In the future, will I still feel this despair? Will I see a meaning for this path I chose?

> **"Will I see a meaning for this path I chose?"**

All in all, I would rather have been enjoying my life instead of living in dread and insecurity all those years. I am writing this to you, future me, so that you can review the situation.

The simple things are what bring me the most enjoyment. Look around. What surrounds you now? What have you chosen?

WRITTEN: April 03, 2005

SENDING: April 03, 2008

Dear FutureMe,

Just got my last email, writ one year ago today. Inspired to write again. G. stopped communicating in February, has been using for who knows how long, was fired, wrecked the car into a jalopy, and is now in the hospital awaiting surgery for who knows what. A. has been removed from his bedside and is in a shelter. J. is clean and sober and is trying to keep rowing her own boat on a clean river and deal with the situation with G. and the family with some honesty and conviction, without compromising her sanity or sobriety.

I do not have a job yet for the coming school year and feel totally demoralized by my loathsome department chair and his tiny, miserable self who chose to hire the infant straight out of school who he can control and intimidate over middle-aged, experienced, talented and passionate me. Working in the public school system is a continual mindfuck: everyone dancing to the mad Big Test Score fiddler while singing about wanting a relevant and meaningful, student-centered, critical thinking curriculum. Trying to dance to two different tunes makes for broken legs. I'm tired, but love teaching teenagers, god help me, and don't want to do anything else. I am fighting like hell to stay optimistic. Medication helps. It's too pathetic for words.

> "I am happy to have the tenderhearted boys in eyelashes and glitter flittering in and out of the house."

I can't say I want out of my earth suit, however I still want less of my earth suit.

R. is a totally, absurdly self-absorbed 17 year old. She is constantly admiring herself in any reflective surface. She is probably failing all her classes and will probably be a beauty school dropout. I refuse to battle her everyday over school, and will not claim her failure in any way, anymore. At least she is not out doing drugs and sleeping around. And she is kind, for the most part, to me and to others. She seems to be keeper of the lonely and gender-confused teenagers at our schools. I am happy to have the tenderhearted boys in eyelashes and glitter flittering in and out of the house. They sometimes bring me a flower or some chocolate: tiny treasures as acknowledgment of my acceptance and celebration of their struggling selves. Better them than het. boys with an agenda drooling over R. She is just not ready for that, and is afraid of their advances. It is far easier being

"Queen of the Queers", where the boys want her only for her friendship and makeup expertise.

Time for coffee and the garden. Be well, current and future me. Remember to breathe, stay hydrated, show up, and such.

My arms are around me.

Love,
Me

WRITTEN: June 18, 2006
SENT: November 18, 2006

Dear FutureMe,

I hope that when you get this email, you will either have stopped writing poetry, or have started writing good poetry. For example:

In the murky water of the pond
The ducklings swim in silence
They swim
In small circles
Not by effort, will, nor decision
By fate, and fortune's hand
For these ducklings,
So small, so innocent,
Have all recently had at least one leg violently wrenched from its socket
In a horrific accident
This accident was strange
Bizarre
Gruesomely hilarious

It involved a tricycle,
Two beach balls,
And a dead goat.
Why had fortune
Dealt these ducklings
Such a cruel hand of life?—
No-one knows.
In the murky water of the pond
The ducklings swim in silence

This is crap.

Kind regards,
~L.

p.s. When you get this, you will be fourteen. Presumably your complexion
will still resemble the Painted Desert in Arizona, but…a man can dream.

WRITTEN: May 25, 2006
SENT: May 25, 2007

I'm drunk, and I'm sure you expect that I'm going to be drunk at this
point. So far, um, well, you should be ready for med school.

I wish I could promise you a rose garden. I wish I could promise you anything at all. You have one more year of prereqs before you're a doctor.

I have no idea what's coming to you. I might tell my therapist (she BET-
TER be gone by now!) that I wrote myself an email. For the future.

i wonder if my head voice is more mature. i wonder if i'm a smarter man.
i wonder if i get it, now. am i faking medicine? am i faking everything?

hey, the "faking everything" should be a flag that nothing's very interesting in here. but in all honesty: i know i'm a fascinating man. this decision clinched it. and now? what do i do? am i still doctor-bound? … probably, if i know my history. i'm stubborn.

as i pee, i need to think of a good closing. WOW is my apartment a shithole (stop making your apartment a shithole).

oh who am I now?

love
i really do love you. more than you love me.

WRITTEN: June 02, 2006
SENT: June 02, 2007

> "I really do love you.
> More than you love me."

Dear FutureMe,

I wish the e-mail-writing thing would also work the other way around so that you could tell me what to say when someone asks "Where do you picture yourself in ten years?" in a job interview. But obviously this would tear up the fabric of time and space, the world would explode and the apocalyptic riders would come and bring death, famine, pestilence and war among us … except for the fact that the latter already happened. As I am left without the means to destroy the universe as we know it, I will try to keep you entertained by telling you what I think will happen in ten years from 2003.

[job interview version] In ten years from now I picture myself in a high management position abroad. After working for a couple of years, I completed my dissertation in less than a year, so that people had to call me doctor and to respect me even though I am young and a woman. I have a loving family with an overly bright kid which does calculus while watching Sesame Street and a husband that supports my career, i.e. cooks and does the laundry. By marrying, I got rid of my unpronounceable family name which made introductions a terrible ordeal. Combined with the fact that I changed my first name so that my correspondence isn't addressed to 'Mr. X' all the time, I will have the positive side-effect that none of the people that I knew in the past can track me down and beg for money because they chose to be poor scientists or artists. [job interview version]

> **"By marrying, I got rid of my unpronounceable family name which made introductions a terrible ordeal."**

And now the 'What I really think will happen' version:

[real version] In ten years emails will be obsolete. Therefore you, FutureMe, will never get this little letter. You however will not be bothered by never receiving this email because there will be a lot of robots which serve your every need and desire (… well, maybe not every desire …). Moreover, robots also do all the thinking for mankind so that you can just hang out in your massage chair and do nothing more than to exist. Lucky bastard. [real version]

Yours faithfully,
A.

WRITTEN: September 27, 2003
SENDING: September 27, 2013

158

Dear FutureMe,

Hi. It's June 2006 me. To start, right now you are a little champ when it comes to being a beer-o and savouring (technically) the last moments of teenage stupidity. But FutureMe, please, I hope you have figured out how to not say mean things about people, because for the most part you aren't really an asshole. Unless FutureMe is an asshole. In that case, fuck you, FutureMe.

Hmm. I also hope that you have managed to figure out how to have a relationship that isn't spectacularly bad, also. I'm really sorry, though, FutureMe, if you haven't figured this one out yet. I'll do my best to help, but I can't control the future or anything.

Remember how amazing the view was out of the window of the living room facing the construction site and the Deutsch Bank building? Oh my goodness. June 2006 me also really likes drinking tea as a means to avoid cleaning up the complete mess made while trying to sort out a bedroom.

But we'll talk soon. I need to start cleaning house, for real—the subletter is coming in 6 hours. Wish me luck!

WRITTEN: June 25, 2006
SENDING: June 25, 2008

> "But FutureMe, please, I hope you have figured out how to not say mean things about people, because for the most part you aren't really an asshole."

So girl. im really worried about you right now because you dont believe in god. you dont care about heaven or hell. it doesnt even exist. if god was real, then this world would not be in this condition. but currently you want to go actively seek out a fellowship to make some new friends and hang with a new crowd.

> "If God was real, then this world would not be in this condition."

i guess 2005 really was a shitty year, now that i think about it. you went to berkeley, met a loser, screwed up your grades, got on academic probation. you made the foolish decision of joining a good for nothing sorority in which the catty girls screwed u over in the end. you were horribly dumped by a mofo and then you went back to him. then even after all that you even tried to be friends with him. this time in june you BETTER NOT be as foolish as you were back then. man. im at a loss for words.

you dont believe in god right now but i think secretly inside you want to but you just dont know how. has this improved?

why else was it shitty? u were screwed over by your friend who is now your roommate. shes a fat bitch by the way, and i hope you never have to see her again. u currently have an ad on craigslist right now for a roommate. i hope you find one so you can move the hell out of there and into a beautiful place like W. shes a fat bitch who is also a pathological liar. you are better than her and should not submit yourself to having to live with a devil like her.

basically at this point in your life, you have concluded that all girls are bitches, guys just want ass and they are all jerks, and god doesnt exist.

you dont know if you can survive spring semester and want to live at the library, or at least some kind of study venue so you can succeed.

but do you really not believe in god? you are so torn right now so i hope the truth is somehow revealed to you this semester in one way or another.

love,
me

WRITTEN: January 11, 2006
SENT: May 30, 2006

Hey me.

I decided to write this because I just got one in my GMail inbox from last year. I didn't even say anything worthwhile. In fact, most of it was just me ranting about some girl named B., who I had totally forgotten about since.

Gee, I wonder why I forgot about her. Possibly because I really fell in love with the most amazing girl on the planet, that's definite. Hopefully you know who I

"Looking back at that other letter, the one from 2005, I wrote that I loved B. Um, that is so not true."

am talking about, but, if something has happened, I am talking about M. She's the most amazing person I have ever met, and she is the first love of my life.

Looking back at that other letter, the one from 2005, I wrote that I loved B. Um, that is so not true. In the short time of one year, I figured out what the word love actually means. And, I didn't have that for B. I don't really remember much of what happened, but I still know that I didn't have LOVE for her.

Love is a huge word, and being truly in love with M. has made me realize that she is indeed my first love, and I am so happy for that, because I know I will remember her for the rest of my life, and I know that there is no one else on earth that I would want to remember for that long.

It's already been ten weeks, and I know for a fact that they have been the best ten weeks of my life. I am really in love with her. And I love it. I look into the future, and see her next to me. Everyday. I know, that's probably pretty unlikely, but. I don't care. I think about that. She is who I want to be with.

Forever.

Hopefully, by reading this, you are happy. If you are happy, congratulations on two years with an amazing girl.

If you aren't, well, I know we are still best friends. And I couldn't think of a better best friend.

WRITTEN: July 02, 2006
SENDING: April 18, 2008

Dear FutureMe,

A year ago today you were a little lonely, frustrated, unhealthy and sad. Up to that point, 2006 had not been so good to you. As you wrote this, you had a headache, a back ache, a sore neck, a wad of gauze in your shorts, fingers that smelled of cigarette smoke, only a single Scottish pound in your wallet, and your dog had farted while he rested on the floor next to you. You were broke. You were bored. You were trapped.

Now you are in a much better position. If you don't believe me, move back in with your mother.

Very truly yours,
You

WRITTEN: January 16, 2006
SENT: January 16, 2007

---

hi,

i bet you are looking back on this day and thinking, what the hell? i am such a loser. a year ago i was really stupid, i am soooo smart now, what could i have known then? ha ha ha. well you know what? shut up futureme, you're a jerk. listen to how smart you used to be.

here are the things that you must must do.

lose weight, seriously, lose all that fat because nothing tastes good enough to be

"... being manorexic is for loser retards with self-esteem issues."

worth being 5 pounds heavier. make sure you take care of your body. but don't be unhealthy about it, being manorexic is for loser retards with self esteem issues.

on that topic, get rid of your self esteem issues. you don't have to be someone else for people to like you, even though i think so right now. i hope

163

that all of that is done with, a year from now. maybe you managed to stay friends, that would be cool. there's no real way to get out scot free, but try not to burn bridges. these people are cool.

work hard!!! i never work hard, but you should.

make friends, smile at people and say hello. don't worry about what they might think about you, only losers worry about that. if they don't like you for who you are, then too fricken bad. act to them like you'd act around your best friend. you're comfortable and you're in control. you're cool.

don't stress about things you can't change. i'm serious, if you can't change it then make the best of it because there's really no point in getting an ulcer over that crap.

> "Work hard!!! I never work hard, but you should."

DANCE! no one cares if you look like a retard!

you know what you need to do right now? this very second? call your grandma. do it. maybe even dad. maybe you don't understand what it means to them to keep in touch with you, but i'm sure it's worth the 15 minutes out of your day.

lastly, don't be so long winded. nobody likes to read 15 paragraph e-mails to their futureselves.

—L.

WRITTEN: July 09, 2006
SENT: July 09, 2007

Dear FutureMe,

Here's what you have to wear this year. Get a big novelty gift tag, or t-shirt, or whatever, and write: "To Women, From God" on it.

Because you're God's gift to women.

Never forget that.

XOXO

D.

WRITTEN: June 29, 2006
SENT: October 25, 2006

Dear FutureMe,

Right now I'm really lost and undecisive about a lot of things. I hope this will provide you insight for whatever you/we may have to endure in the near/distant future. I know you know that right now I am gay and closeted. You also now that right now I am having a relationship with a guy who's in college, but even though I'm still in high school, we love each other a lot. This brings me to my letter for you. No matter what happens in the next few months/years never forget this time in your life … My family is a bunch of conservative religious bastards who hate anything that even so much as hints disobedience to the bible. My boyfriend, who lives about a two hour drive away, doesn't want me to just pick the nearest college by him and go there. Between you and me, I haven't even met him, but he is attractive and very sweet … He's smart too. I wish I hadn't made that wish so many months ago to have a boyfriend because now my wish has been granted, but at the cost of no longer wanting to go to my dream college. You see, he lives in a city far away from my ideal college. However, he attends a college that is acknowledged around the world! So was my dream school, but he doesn't go to that one.

> "My boyfriend, who lives two hours away, doesn't want me to just pick the nearest college and go there. Between you and me, I haven't even met him …"

You can see my predicament … I'm a closeted gay who has a long distance boyfriend and is on the threshold of making the most influential decision of my life, possibly … I've entertained the thought/fear that we may not work out and I abandoned my dream for naught, but I have hope … I wish I do get accepted to his school … that way EVERYTHING will work out! I'll be away from my family, I'll be with him and I'll be happy! I've already been accepted to my dream school (which is slightly selective and competitive), so there may be a chance I'll get into his school as well … I can only hope … As I said earlier, I am still in the closet (by the way so is he) and I face hidden

166

discrimination almost on a daily basis. My friends deem things 'gay' if it is not good to them and I see the marriage issues on television almost every day. I just wish people would wake up and realize that humans are capable of love and that if they just so happen to love someone of the same gender, that's okay! Homosexuality wasn't a problem in the world a thousand years ago! It all has to do with religion.

Don't forget to get yourself checked out for emotional/psychological problems while you're away. I'm sure stayin this long in the closet wasn't good for you. Also don't forget… I believe he really DOES LOVE me! Just because he doesn't call when you like doesn't mean he doesn't care! Remember what he said? He doesn't want to be the cause of you not getting a good education! He wouldn't say that if he didn't love you/me! Don't take it for granted and DON'T abuse him… I love him… now at least. Remember, he was your dream come true and if I'm right (hope-fully), your dream isn't done being realized yet! Don't give up and don't worry about not knowing what to major for in college, it'll come to you in time… I'm glad I stumbled across this because I believe this will make all the difference later… love YOU always…

Past-self

P.S. You're eighteen today. I hope he's there with you. Tell him I love him and that I will continue to love him even if we don't work out… give him a kiss… for me… bye

WRITTEN: January 21, 2006
SENT: March 22, 2006

Okay, let me start this letter off with this: YOU SUCK.

Why? Because the time is 11:00pm, and you (I? you? or perhaps the Royal We) have (y)our first exam tomorrow. Maths. And well, true to your legendary procrastination ways, you have not studied at all. You're ruining my life. I'm ruining your life. I wonder if I'll ruin your life? Time for some changes huh? Yeah, change is a good thing.

> **"Get over this salesman mentality, where you're just talking shit to people and would not remember a conversation if your life depended on it."**

I was reading about the ego the other day (instead of studying, farrrout) and basically, there's an idea that the ego consists of a series of salient/recent impressions/experiences. And thus, the ego is never the same from one moment to the next. And so, by the time you're reading this, you are truly a "you" and no longer "me," for I would have been eroded away by the tides of time. Yes, in fact, the "I" which we refer to ourselves, without even thinking, would have died thousands of deaths.

Anyways, enough of the small talk. Let's get down to business. There are a few things I expect you to have done by the time you are reading this:

1. Maintain at least a Distinction average. I know, a bit selfish of me considering I'm going to be a major drag on your distinction average, but seriously. I guess the issue here is I hope you've become a more responsible person, who is able to both play hard and work hard. I know we can do it, we've done it before.

168

2. Get a fucking boyfriend. Geez. Love is so beautiful, and I'm beginning to wonder maybe beauty is not going to drop down on my lap while I sit here idly. That means being active. And yes, that means being social.

3. God, I hope you've become more of a social person. Get over this salesman mentality I have right now, where you're just talking shit to people and would not remember a conversation (or a name) if your life depended on it. Most people are good, and fun, and nice, and it takes time to get to know them.

4. Doing well in piano. All this nail cutting better pay off huh? I am working hard. You know how badly you want this, to be able to stop your own heart jay chou style. =D

5. Have a better relationship with the family. Yes, love sometimes needs to be shown.

Oh look at that, 11:53. And suddenly I am ohsotired, because tomorrow I have an exam and I should be studying. Maybe I shouldn't have stayed up to 3am for the past week or so.

> **"Equilibrium is still a beautiful thing, unless you've found a theory which usurps equilibrium in its wondrousness."**

Gosh, there are so many things which I am confused about right now. You know, the eternal questions. Superficiality, consumerism, versus the ideal. I guess one needs to strike a balance. Equilibrium is still a beautiful thing, unless you've found a theory which usurps equilibrium in its wondrousness.

Writing this has made me depressed. There are so many things which I have been avoiding to confront. Instead, I pacify and waste myself away on the internet. It's like a tv now, just a glowing screen of mindless meaninglessness. Have strength.

To Greatness, and Godlidom.

Yours narcissistically,
You. (me)

WRITTEN: June 19, 2006
SENT: June 19, 2007

Dear FutureMe,

im 16. school sucks balls. i hate it but i finally got most of my Cs up to Bs. im wearing a black shirt with a skeleton on the front and it says misfits on the bottom. my pants are dark dark blue and pretty baggy. im also wearing a black leather belt and my hair is about 2-3 inches long. im almost 6 ft tall and i weigh a little over 200 lbs. its sunday today, i got so damn stoned yesterday. it was fun. m. was sick though so he had to stop cuz he was gonna puke. i hope i never get caught with weed, that would suck, slap myself now if i ever did. slap myself now if i dont smoke it anymore. good friends are: t., m., d. favorite bands: nofx, lagwagon, misfits, tsunami bomb, guttermouth, mad caddies, mars volta, bouncing souls, and dropkick murphys. i play guitar and listen to music and play video games and smoke weed and go to concerts and see movies with my friends. dont wanna write anymore. live well

WRITTEN: November 17, 2003
SENDING: August 02, 2008

Well, hello! And happy birthday! I'm at an interesting turning point right now. I'm just about to graduate from high school and move on into the wide world of college! I've recently come to a lot of conclusions about myself, but I'm not sure how many of them will stay. I just discovered an online community of fellow asexuals to talk to. I'm also contemplating what to do about my gender identity/neutrois, leaning towards male. I don't know whether I'll transition or not.

WRITTEN: April 10, 2006

SENDING: May 10, 2010

1491 days

So … hi there. Apparently, you made it to age 18 without dying as a result of doing something really fucking stupid. Congrats. Happy birthday. Now go get me a pack of fuckin' cigarettes, bitch.

I'm just kidding. Really. Do you still have a fucked-up sense of humor? Do you still think it's fucked-up? What are you like now, anyway? Are you still a total music whore? What happened to your job at McDonald's? Do you ever talk to L. anymore? Or the other people you met online? What about M. and G. and C. and T. and everyone else from school? Have you come out to everyone yet? Did anything ever happen with D. the way you dreamed it would?

I'm sorry if something I've asked has upset you somehow, disappointed you by reminding you of something you used to long for but gave up on. I didn't mean to do that, I guess I was just curious. Or are you okay with giving up on certain aspirations because you find new ones to replace them.

No matter how amazing (or, I guess, horrible) your life is now, I just don't want you to forget the way you are now. Don't forget midnights at the beach, long AIM conversations about nothing with the girl who loves you best, SAT prep, seven-hour shifts at McDonald's, and how it feels to be sitting here right now, dreaming of what's gonna happen next.

WRITTEN: July 30, 2006
SENDING: July 02, 2008

Dear FutureMe,

i want so badly to <b> love him <b>
i want to love him and marry him
but i can't, because he's not christian
i had never realized until now how restrictive that sounds
i'm never really free to love who i want
the world is not mine

despite the fact that the last christian boy i was with got us naked in bed
and did some unspeakable things

despite the fact that the one before that who sings & plays in church and is a youth music pastor would lose all self control alot of nights & our bodies would get crazy and he would make me feel like crap

despite the fact that these christian boys were sometimes real assholes— reckless with my feelings & heart (don't be reckless with other people's hearts, don't put up with people who are reckless with yours)

now i have found a georgeous boy who treats me beautifully, who looks at me as though he's never seen a girl before and i'm the most amazing discovery, who holds me (and loves to hold me) but doesn't lose self control, who respects & loves his family, who doesn't complain, who doesn't lose patience, who loves me.

> "I want to love him and marry him. But I can't, because he's not Christian."

but he doesn't believe in God.

—the one maker/breaker as far as my family/friends are concerned. the ONE THING i've been taught since i was a little girl that is THE deal-breaker.

it's devastating
i'm in love
and it just can't happen
but i'm in love!
I'M IN LOVE

(and i should worry later [but i can't stop worrying now])

WRITTEN: July 01, 2006
SENT: July 01, 2007

What's up girl!!! How ya doin? I hope you are okay? Did you drop that loser, get out of that situation & not hook up w/ another bad guy? Please say you did?! Please? Listen if you haven't, here's the last pep talk: He's no good for you, no matter what he says or how he acts when he wants something, actions speak louder than words & he's done more than enough to show you that you would be wasting your time to stick it out w/ him. He doesn't love you, and probably not anybody but his own self. Please!!! I love you, be strong!!! You know you are stronger than that. Bottom line—he sucks!!! Run, run, run as fast as you can!!!

"Run, run, run as fast as you can!!!"

WRITTEN: January 30, 2006
SENT: January 30, 2007

Dear FutureMe,

try these numbers

3, 21, 33, 35, 42, 5

I'm going to be rich rich rich … Oh wait … I think this is backwards … mailing myself the numbers in the future is no good … I'm dumb dumb dumb.

Hey Future self … send me the lottery numbers … I'll make us rich rich rich …

WRITTEN: July 16, 2006
SENDING: July 16, 2010

This is your past self reminding your future self to try something crazy.

Your assignment for today: Call a total stranger (preferably someone lonely, like an elderly person or a (?!?) prisoner) and talk to them. Their spirits must be lifted before you're allowed to hang up the phone.

WRITTEN: December 20, 2005
SENT: June 27, 2006

189 days

Dear FutureMe,

What a week. My sobriety/clean date is November 13, 2004. I am an alcoholic. I attend Alcoholics Anonymous meetings. I am an addict. I attend Narcotics Anonymous meetings. This sometimes becomes an issue, not recently. 'One program, many fellowships' were words spoken that resounded in my heart. I thought I would give a bit of background before going into my week. In A.A. and N.A., there is a suggestion to ask someone to be your "sponsor." This person is to aid you in your journey through the Twelve Steps. My sponsor just

> # "My prognosis for any attempts at reality-based romance is grim."

celebrated 10 years of sobriety, this evening.

Last Friday, I 'gave a lead'. This is an archaic term describing a meeting where there is only one person speaking for the entirety of the meeting, sharing his/her experience, strength, and hope. I have been asked five times to do this in my short period of time in the program. Each time, I find I undergo an intense two week period of extreme pain following these sharing adventures. I believe this is a direct result of ripping away the unending layers of masks or walls that shield and trap me, psychicly. When I have achieved some level of alignment with the will of a Higher Power and then choose to voice my impression of that force at work within me, change occurs. Rapid, painful growth. This week I have been angst-ridden, resentful, and living in a fear-based fantasy world. I have not acted upon these emotions, thanks to effective brainwashing. Lost within a Bermuda Triangle of self-obsession, I perceive productive days as horrific wastes of time. My attitude creates a self-loathing and sense of inadequacy. Thus, I plunge deeper into the morass.

In the last few days these self-destructive impulses have given way to a melancholy, complete with tear-rimmed eyes. This has been beneficial. I see progress and understand I am currently running a complete gamut of emotions. The saving grace of a power greater than myself coupled with a reliance upon suggestions given by those who have traveled this road before, leads me to not pick up the first drink. It matters not the emotions I process these days, what matters is the choices in the physical plane I make.

I am altering my prayer life. I ask for help developing character. I remain committed to kneeling or lying face down, when in a prayerful act. I pledge each day to not drink alcohol or use mind-altering substances. I study in The Big Book of Alcoholics Anonymous. I attend meetings daily, at the very least. I spend quality time with other humans in recovery. This is a plan for the prevention of relapse, given to me by predecessors whom had it handed down to them.

I am beginning to get a firmer grasp on the concept that my inability to form a substantial relationship with a woman is a direct result of the phantasmal 'girlfriends' I carry ahead inside my twisted psyche. I project them on to a human host. I isolate to the deepest, dankest recesses of my mind's eye and grant them audience. I mourn them. I resurrect them. I caress them. I court them. I drunkenly grope them. I seduce them. I relive the domination, the submission. I give them what they want. I take what I need. I abuse them. I empower them. I use them as a means to engage in a sado-masochistic co-dependency with myself. This could prove to be quite troublesome to correct. My prognosis for any attempts at reality-based romance is grim.

I am blessed with a fraction of acceptance, a glimmer of hope. I have started a journey of reconciliation using honesty, open-mindedness, and willingness. Yesterday is history, tomorrow is a mystery, and today is called the present, because that's what it is … A GIFT. I feel confident I will not drink or use drugs today. I am confident that I will continue to grow. I believe that by living life, loving that life, and sharing that love with others I will be led to a greater understanding and acceptance of my role in this grand play.

Love and Service,

WRITTEN: July 31, 2006
SENT: July 31, 2007

Dear FutureMe,

I just broke up with M. a few days ago and am finding it hard not to call him back and apologize for being jealous … But I know it was the right thing to do. We had fun together but he will never be faithful and he made me feel as if I wasn't anything to him. Just a friend with benefits. That hurt the worst because he had asked me to move in with him. He also said he was committed. He lied. So much.

God I just pray I'll never call him back. But I wouldn't bet on it.

WRITTEN: June 23, 2006
SENT: January 01, 2007

192 days

Dear FutureMe,

Are you still loving the one you think you can't have? Why do you think he wouldn't like to go out with you? There's nothing wrong with you, other than your lack of self confidence when it comes to him. You can flirt like there's no tomorrow with him, grab the bull by the balls and ask him out if you haven't already. He wouldn't do all the little things he's done for you over the years if he didn't feel something for you. You only have one chance with him, right here, right now, don't let it fall to the wayside.

"Grab the bull by the balls and ask him out if you haven't already."

WRITTEN: August 01, 2006
SENT: August 01, 2007

Dear FutureMe,

it's taken me a while to sit down and actually write this. busyness, and reluctance to play with fate. destiny, whatever. i am still unsure, but risking it. it is the moment that deserves to be remembered, after all, i want to remember the moments as what i have; what i have had all along.

i know where i'd like to be, i'd like to have traveled across oceans and mountains and volcanoes and made it back home in one piece. i'd like to maybe have written some things i'm really proud of. i'd like to be starting a masters degree and maybe have a little more of a clue about what might be coming. just a little.

struggling as i always do, wrestling with words so i do not end up giving myself a list of dos and don'ts. gold stars and detentions, depending on where i am at the exact moment i receive the email i sent myself a year ago. i cannot possibly know my future self, i don't know what i'll need to hear today-in-the-future more than any other. what wisdom i have now will have been tempered by many other things, more weddings and birthdays and deaths. is it so foolish to want to try to project?

i'll risk sounding young, cynical, naive, crazy. because what i write now is now, deserves to be recorded as such. a moment; photographed, clear, fast-forwarded to this time next year. who knows where i'll be, what i'll be doing, but maybe i need to be reminded of now, of this small epiphany. glimpses of where i came from, a little of the story that took me forward to then. past into present; what you carry always comes with you.

i wrote myself three notes this week. one is post-it containing the words "you are more transparent than you think you are." the others are longer. i talked of changes in season, the tilting autumn sunlight, the crazy weather. i wrote of always waiting for something, caught between looking forward and looking back; a flux of uncertainty. the rain falls quietly, like a lullaby. i think of my story, of other people's stories, the things that make us essentially us. a little crazy. today sees me carrying past and present sadnesses across my chest. unsure, unsteady, waiting, longing to not be waiting. maybe this will makes sense later, next year, tomorrow. who knows, really?

these are moments, moments you can only hold on to, trying not to forget.

happy september 6th 2005, futureme. i hope you're still this crazy.

WRITTEN: September 12, 2004
SENT: September 06, 2005

180

one week in june, summer of 2006

from monday 19th 5:45 a.m. to monday 26th 5:45 a.m. you were so very in love (you never had been before) with an american boy named c.

it felt different and more lovely than any of the others.

you pretended to get married in the airport as the rain poured down before the sun came up and wore little black strings around your fingers and he promised to find you.

(and still, you are a little worried because he is not the one thing your parents require him to be. you're not sure how it could ever be resolved—and so goes almost every tragic love story ever told.)

WRITTEN: June 28, 2006
SENT: June 17, 2007

354 days

Dear FutureMe,

i decided to tell you a secret…
right now.
your breasts are uneven.
are they uneven as you read this?
you like d. s.
did anything ever happen with that?
you miss j. b. and j. a.
have you seen either of them?
you are over suicide.
is that still true?
you don't care what others think of you.
why?

WRITTEN: September 08, 2006
SENT: February 20, 2007

"… don't waste your time, don't marry them, don't spend money on them, just sleep with them …"

Dear FutureMe,

Women, well, they are… impossible, dont waste your time, dont marry them, dont spend money on them, just sleep with them, thats all it comes down too.

If your still doing this in your 38 years of existance, well, to be frank, your the man… and if your doing this to more than five women a month, you wear the serious bling, and own your own plastic surgery clinic, and have the mintest milf receptionist, im goin 2 hav 2 say your the greatest man it the world … oh … and your going to be priminister too, if your not, i hope you are rootin at least 20 women a month … and show clinton how those interns are really done.

Cheer bo

H.

WRITTEN: September 26, 2004

SENDING: January 01, 2024

Dear FutureMe,

As you read this, you're probably sitting in your parents' fancy new house in Vegas. Are they happy? If not, tell them their PastDaughter says smile. I'm sure they're happy. Give them a hug for me.

I hope you've had a good summer. You've graduated college and driven across the country. I hope it was all you thought it was going to be. Did you stand at the Grand Canyon all by yourself? I hope you did. You sure as hell better be packed to go to London. Remember that if you're not, I will never forgive you. I hope you have your plane ticket. I'm sure you're scared. I'm scared for you. But don't be too scared. It's time to go. It's been time to just go for a long time.

As I, your now past self, am writing this to you, you have been drafting an e-mail to T. You probably won't send it, even though last night you drove around listening to the radio, making a tally of the songs that said "yes, send it" and the ones that said "no, do not." You had 5 tallies for yes and 4 for no. And 2 maybes, one of which was a song on WONC's FemFM show that said something about doing it on the bathroom floor. One of the no's was Turning Japanese. I hope you've started to get over it, or

"... think about all the growing up you still have to do. Don't be scared of that. Thank God for that."

have started to live with it, because he don't love you girl, and you never knew him. (The e-mail was classy though, don't be ashamed of it.) If you still think about him, it's ok. You think about him because you never knew him, but don't think sad things. Meet someone and shut up. And look where you are now, you're very far away. Wise up, but don't get too practical.

Have fun in London. Don't be a wimp. And hey, when you get back, get some cash and a decent car and drive to Newfoundland. You've grown up a lot, I can tell, and think about all the growing up you still have to do. Don't be scared of that. Thank God for that.

I love you. I know you'll badmouth me sometimes, and I'm sure I deserve it, but I'm pulling for you. Be good, but not too good.

—D.

WRITTEN: August 03, 2006
SENT: August 03, 2007

---

its easy to be a soldier when u declare your oath, sing Star Spangled Banner before tha president & nation in a sunny day & when they say you're a hero

its hard to be a soldier when you're fightin alone with unknown enemy who knows your every next step, everyone is against you & dont belive your fightin has any sens & you have no more source of strenth you can't comunicate with your leaders nor anybody who may help you

your enemy laught at you & everythin tells you you cannot ever win

you don stop to a soldier when they tear your uniform on you, rape you when you cant defend your honor or kill you

you stop to be a soldier 4ever when u turn to their side

even if for your alliegance you must pay tha price which i wrote up

don blame u coz they killed your friends & say that they did this cuz you didn wanna cooperate with em

President Bush said that if we wouldn fight against em, they would fight against us however

tha more you let em do, tha more they will do

to be a soldier don means only to shoot but to have faith to the end

WRITTEN: May 18, 2006

SENT: June 17, 2006

Dear FutureMe,

Is it your anniversary? If it is, get away from him a.s.a.p. You know you deserve better, and if you have gotten away congrads. You have the whole world at your feet…

PastMe

WRITTEN: July 23, 2006

SENT: November 23, 2006

Dear FutureMe,

On April 11, 2005, the newly elected president of Iraq said he expects that U.S. troops will be gone from his country within two years.

So, it's April 11th 2007 ...

WRITTEN: April 11, 2005
SENT: April 11, 2007

You better be better by now. A month or so ago you sent a final email to C., finalizing no communication, although you seem to suffer in bits and pieces every day, every hour, regardless. You would look for her on the street, wonder what she was doing at night, imagine her with N. in their honeymoon phase ... and all that it involved. She grew instantly distant once she met him ... fucked him on the second date. No therapy or medication would work, although you've been sober for 2 weeks now ...

You were surfing for the first time ... 4 times in one week. You went out with I., and had a very in-depth conversation of sorts. A connection?

At home you were questioning your future, and self worth. Making potential plans for classes in the fall, and an apartment in the somewhat near future. Returning the stupid x-box, and going to meetings 5 times a week.

Lonely, in pain, thinking too much, but knowing, or trying to convince yourself, that it was right. Never right to begin with, I mean 3½ years ... gone like that. And she does what she has always done, into the arms of another man as a substitute for her own lack of self-esteem. Defined by only the man in her life, having no direction in life to begin with (that's where we were similar), and continuing to live in thick denial by claiming that she is "just having fun."

> "But we had something ... what, I don't know and can't define ... and maybe should just stop trying all together."

Why was it then that you were asking about marriage 3 days before you cheated on me? Blackout you called it. Bullshit. And then going crazy insane on me when I threw you out. Was it all worth it? Was our time together really all that bad? I know the drinking was at the end ...

But we had something ... what I don't know and can't define ...

and maybe should just stop trying all together.

Damn it all.

WRITTEN: August 13, 2006
SENT: September 13, 2007

Dear FutureMe,

How are things? Now I am waiting for the plane to arrive. Well in six hours.

This is a tough place in my life. I want to know what you know. Looking back is so easy. So are you divorced, back together, on the road to divorce? Say hi to your daughter for me. That is the toughest in all of this. You no longer want to be with her but your daughter is blessed. You need to tell her that you and her mother love her dearly and that won't change regardless of how you and mom are getting along. Please tell me you're out of your parents' house. It's bad enough that I won't stay in the house any longer but to be back with mom & dad? What is going on there? Can you explain to her yet that you lied? That you played the game because it was safe? The last was so bad, you went for something safe didn't you? You tried hard not to fight because that's all you knew. You don't talk like you should because you are afraid of the truth. You shuddered when the ring was made. You got so drunk the night before the wedding probably in the hopes of pissing someone off. Hell, you cried when you danced with your mother! You hadn't lived in her house in a couple of years! WHY DO YOU CONTINUE TO TRY AND MAKE EVERYONE ELSE HAPPY BESIDES YOURSELF? I hope things are going well with everyone else. I hope you have found happiness. You did a bad thing. You will have to pay in tears and heartbreak. This is a very painful lesson.

"You shuddered when the ring was made. You got so drunk the night before the wedding ..."

What makes us love someone? What is it about someone that doesn't share a single common trait with you that makes you nuts? Why is someone who never argues with you and shares all the same interests not the right person for you? What is that bond that is created with some and not with others? Hopefully you find this note to be the ramblings of a bad moment in your life and you are making an effort to bring your life around. Say hi to mom and dad.

Take care.

WRITTEN: February 16, 2006
SENT: February 16, 2007

Dear FutureMe,

Are you still thinking that by having sex with a man, he will fall head over heels in love with you? That by having sex with him, it will make him want to be with you? You need to stop doing that right now! It doesn't work that way! He should love you for who you are, not how well you screw him!

WRITTEN: August 01, 2006
SENT: December 31, 2006

152 days

Did you marry her or not? I hope you did and that you figured out where the two of you will live and that you are happy and that you still have sex and, more importantly, still make time to do nothing but hold each other. I know we're going to come to a decision this year. I hope it's one that works for both of us.

I also hope you figured out how to cope with the health problems that are coming back now, as I write this. All that crap about it being cool to grow old doesn't mean much when you feel the way I do right now and know what might come. Are you exercising regularly? I can't seem to keep it up.

I'll bet you've cut your hair by now. I'm already thinking about it. Dad's hairline is nice … but it doesn't work with the length I've got now. Oh, well. That had to come. I know, the chicks dig the long hair. But short-haired and good looking is better than longhaired and sketchy looking.

Are you still at the same place? (Depends on whether or not you've moved, I guess.) Heh, do you still have this email address? Talk about coping with bullshit.

I'm staring at this screen wondering what else to say to you but you know I've never been good at planning or even thinking for the future. I'm sorry about that. I know we want to look somewhere else for an explanation. But, really, it's you. Me, that is.

Hope your birthday was great.

"45"

p.s. I hope you've stopped doing those ordeals. I'm trying to quit but it's like a drug. I guess we've never been strong.

WRITTEN: August 03, 2006
SENDING: August 01, 2011

I am one ugly motherfucker. Why did I have to look so ugly? My face is like shit, because I am ugly. I know I am ugly, and will always be ugly. No girl likes me, they all say they look at personality, but I know that's bullshit. Oh well, I don't care. I'm going to grow up and be a rich man that lives all by myself because girls don't like me because I'm ugly. I shouldn't blame them because I'm ugly, I'm just ugly. Oh well. My parents don't even know I like girls, even if a girl did like me, I wouldn't be able to do anything with them because of parents like mine. Fuck, I kinda hate my life right now. I'm reading the book Go Ask Alice. Just thought I'd say that. My shoulder hurts, I hurt it. Man, me and S. are the 2 ugliest friends in the school. I'm serious, we 2 met each other because we are fucking uglier than the other 2100 students. I will never go to a fucking prom because my parents won't let me and I'm damn ugly. Oh well, I'll tell them I'm going to a movie or something, and I'll take a blow up doll with me and dance with the blow up doll. Man, no girl likes me, I'm fucking ugly. But come on, I'm a world champion powerlifter too. And I'm really nice, but I know I'm ugly. Oh well, at least lifting makes me feel happy, and I get respect from lots of men. I'm really nice, but I guess I'm not the type that girls will like. Oh well, and my parents are making things worse, 'cause if someone ever does, 1 in 10 million, couldn't do anything with them since my parents don't let. Oh well, I guess I'll be a lonely man with a big nice house and nice cars. That'll make me happy. I'll also have nice motor-cycles and everything!

> ## "And I'm really nice, but I know I'm ugly."

WRITTEN: November 23, 2003
SENT: May 10, 2006

Dear FutureMe,

I am 15 years old. Couple days ago L. told me to kiss her, but I didn't because I got carried away in a conversation and because I'm an ugly little kid. Oh well, it doesn't matter. A. makes me feel good. Sometimes I just want to kiss her and go to bed with her. You know what I mean, not in a way of fuck her, but with love. But then again I'm so in love with L. I wish I can have her.

My biceps are 13 inches, benching about 175 raw probably, 155 for 3 sets of 5. Anyways me, I want to see what I was a couple years ago. 2 Years I guess. I used to wack off like once a week, now it was like 2 times a day for like a week. I don't know why. But I didn't yesterday, I want to quit. I dressed up like a girl with J. and C. last school year. Uhhh, I don't know. When you get this S., you fucking ugly ass mother fucking hoe. You know you're ugly. Just read it and see if you're the same. Hopefully you're hot now, but oh well.

WRITTEN: September 17, 2003
SENT: September 17, 2005

Hello my friend.

5 years ago you were:

Dealing with a lot of stuff. You just attended your 10 yr. h.s. reunion. Surprisingly you had an awesome time, it was good to catch up with so many old friends. You also lost 23 lbs and 9" in 2 months in preparation for the reunion. Way to kick some ass! Currently you are 175lbs, but there's still room for improvement even if everyone thinks you're looking fit. Are you still fit or did you turn into a fatty?

Remember the day after the reunion? You had the hardest day you had ever breathed. L. met you at Starbucks and the two of you had the time of your life for 5 hours, talking about the unfathomable connection you both shared. At times both of you just stopped and stared into each other's eyes, never doubting what the other was thinking. It was miserable delight. You knew at the end you would say goodbye forever, knowing that she still loves you even though she's married. Being an upstanding woman she decided it was too hard to just be friends if she was married. Do you remember the way you cried in your room that night? The next day? And the day after that? And now here it is her birthday and you still can't shake her from your registers. What was the purpose of it all? I don't know but I hope you have figured it out in five years. If so, be sure to come back and tell me because right now, my head is swimming in muck.

From,
Your 28 yr. old self

WRITTEN: August 04, 2006
SENDING: August 03, 2011

> **"The Army has your body fighting for them; your mind must defend itself."**

Dear FutureMe,

It has been a long, hard road
I'm sure. Ultimitly it will all be worth it. I am so scared right now. Don't forget about that damn k./a. sandwich waiting for you back in the states, you deserve it. If there are no cool people anywhere—it is time to go to Xenotopia. Make a picture of S. and J. playing chess, make it totally sweet. The Army has your body fighting for them; your mind must defend itself.

WRITTEN: November 17, 2003
SENT: November 17, 2004

You've been spending a lot of time trying to conceal your wrist. It's starting to heal but you wish it weren't. You have been lying to everyone you care about (best friend, mom and L.) about it. You know what happened there … It's NOT just a scratch. You lock yourself in the bathroom and dig in with a safety pin until you bleed and you can breathe again.

It's funny because when you do it, you leave the medicine cabinet door open so you can't see your face in the mirror. Because if you see your face, you cry. You sometimes want to shout what it really is to your bff but she keeps on talking about how she's way past cutting and self harm because it's stupid. You don't want to BE STUPID or act like a preteen going through a phase. You just want someone to want to stop you.

> "Normal teens don't have to make themselves bleed so they can breathe again."

For God's sake you're fucking 18 in a week, and you are obsessed with some safety pin … You were so scared because one day you needed to so bad so you locked yourself in the bathroom and looked in the cabinet and it wasn't there. Someone took your safety pin. You spent the entire day looking for it, thinking about it. In the end you used a smaller safety pin you found. You're still afraid someone knows. Your doctor was wrong, you lied to him and he told your mother it's normal teenage stuff not depression or anything else. Normal teens don't have to make themselves bleed so they can breathe again.

You have to stop on your own, because you can't keep on and you can't tell.

WRITTEN: September 08, 2005
SENT: December 08, 2005

Dear FutureMe,

Do you want to thank me, or strangle me for my decisions? Have you any regrets brewing in your gut that I am to blame for? You know that I tried my hardest, and my best to make your life easyer … often at my own discomfort and downfall. All I'm asking for is a little respect, maybe a moment of silence for your fallen PastMe, who is no more and who sacrificed so much for your freedom.

It's Remember-ME day.

Love and hope,
PastMe

WRITTEN: November 19, 2003
SENT: November 12, 2005

Dear FutureMe,

I don't really know why this seems like the only way that you'll hear the truth. There is nothing wrong with you. You are a wonderful person—inside and out. I guess the first time I sent a letter I thought that maybe this would all be over. Sometimes I feel like I will be sick forever. For a while I am fine, and then my thoughts get desperate. I feel sick and fat and ugly and fucked up.

In case you glazed over it last time—THERE IS NOTHING WRONG WITH YOU! At this moment, as I write this, I am a size 8. I have the love of a wonderful man, and a beautiful daughter who is growing and seeing the world around her.

Do you want your beautiful little girl to do this to herself? If you can't get better for you—do it for her. Do it for everyone else who is watching you fall. I am sending this just after you complete your 12 week program. As always, relying on an external force to hopefully get you through this.

Quit starving yourself. Quit denying yourself the love that you deserve. Quit starving yourself to keep out emotion. Food isn't the enemy. And neither is your body.

Purge yourself of negativity. Starve yourself of sadness. CHOOSE YOUR PATH! What has happened in the past is only an opportunity to grow and learn and change. You fail when you stay still. Quit staying still.

"The only play that matters is the next play."

The only play that matters is the next play.

I am making this a public letter. I want anyone who sees this to know the truth about me—even if they don't know who I am. Maybe someone is reading these letters, searching for an answer, as I was. The answer is there. Inside you. I am bulimic. I starve myself because I think I am fat. At 135 lbs, I was taking laxatives to keep me thin. I wore a size 4. I was eating less than 500 calories a day. Working out more than 600 calories a day. And I was getting sicker by the day. I am in recovery now, and haven't had such negative behavior. But believe me, those demons never let me forget that they aren't far behind. If you, like me, suffer from self-abusive behavior—get help. It will kill you someday. Physical pain isn't nearly as bad as emotional pain. Trust me, your scars will heal on the outside. But until you can heal the inside, you'll always hurt. And it isn't worth it. If you are reading these letters, looking for answers—you have to see that you must know that there is a problem. If you can't afford help, tell someone who can be trusted. Tell your family or a friend who doesn't support your self-abuse. Tell a priest. Tell a guy on the street. Tell everyone. The more you talk, the more people who care will watch and take notice. And it won't be easy. But you can get better. Doing what is right is almost NEVER doing what is easy.

Remember that. Remember me. Remember that the only play that matters is the next play.

WRITTEN: August 29, 2006
SENT: November 27, 2006

Dear Future Me,

well today i think i got with B. but i'm not sure. its 5:08 but like just turned 5:08 right while i was typing i took caffeine earlier but it didn't do very much i don't think the cat is standing next to me and i think he wants to go outside but fuck him he's a cat i got my controller to work on my PC so i can play cs and DOD and halo with a ps2 esque controller. today i trimmed my pubes…

well thats about all the random info i can put in one message to me in the future i hope this finds me well

when i get this i should be 18 i hope this server is still running because i know ill "lol" if and or when i recieve this

love (and other such bs)
—J. from 2006

WRITTEN: June 26, 2006
SENDING: June 26, 2018

Telling myself what to do in the future is just plain stupid. All the wisdom I have now is not going to help me in the future. In fact, I should be sending emails to me in the past to avoid certain mistakes. Make that service, smart guys.

WRITTEN: February 10, 2006
SENDING: February 01, 2010

1452 days

Dear FutureMe,

It is 7:18pm, Wednesday, August 9, 2006.

I've been thinking about a lot of things lately. About T. (you do remember the guy you met on the airpark that was in jail, right?). I've been wondering if it's really going to go anywhere. We've been writing back and forth for a little while now, and you better still have those letters! Always save everything!

Are you still taking pictures? I hope so! Take pictures all the time. You remember when H. L. was murdered … you didn't have any recent pictures of her. I am still sad about her death. The court date is in September for her "alleged" killer.

Have you moved out of your mother's house???!!! If not, pack your shit, and leave IMMEDIATELY!!! It doesn't matter where you go.

Have you found a tall, handsome cowboy? I've been checking them out lately and DAMN there are some fine white guys around here.

I still live with mom now. I work at Hertz, cleaning cars. It's hella hot down here in Louisiana.

Hunt much lately? I got my first deer last year … 7 point. Big fella' he was. If you haven't went hunting in the past 2 years, get back into it. It's a great time to relax and get away. Have kids? Find a sitter.

Still broke? Buy a lottery ticket. Use numbers 7, 13, 11, 01, 30, 21. I hope you get lucky! You probably won't, but it's worth a shot.

This is where I end this letter. I hope you've found the love of your life. If not … he will come. I hope you've found a job you enjoy. If not, set out to find it. I hope you're happy. If not, just breathe, and remember that someone out there loves you besides yourself.

WRITTEN: August 09, 2006
SENDING: November 01, 2014

> **"Buy a lottery ticket. Use numbers 7, 13, 11, 01, 30, 21."**

Sorry I ruined your life.

Oh, and a Happy 30th Birthday!

WRITTEN: October 02, 2005
SENDING: September 24, 2012

"Please live long enough to read this e-mail. If you die, please die in combat."

dear future self:

please live long enough to read this e-mail. if you die, please die in combat. it's the way you wanted to go.

whatever you see and do, don't forget why you enlisted.

remember the destruction that decision caused. remember the fights, the tears, the promises, the worries, the determination.

at the time of this writing, you lived in the greatest country in the world. i hope you still do.

remember who you were, aged seventeen.

whatever shitty duty you're assigned, do it with vigor and pride.

if you lost a limb, a buddy, youth, friends—remember that freedom is always worth it.

freedom is always worth it.

faith.

WRITTEN: October 21, 2005
SENT: October 21, 2007

Dear FutureMe,

For two days you've been chatting and exchanging increasingly explicit pics with a woman you've never met. She's played with herself on her webcam. You've been more excited than you've been for a long time. She says she wants you. The thought excites you beyond belief.

But you're married, to a great woman, so why are you even thinking about doing this? Why are you even talking to this woman? She's admitted she's fucking at least three other married guys. Is that what turns you on? She's so easy and it's dangerous and you shouldn't be doing it. Your own life is pretty dull and this feels exciting. You know you should be doing something to spice up your life with your wife … but she's always so knackered from work, and sex is a rare event. You want this new woman so bad. Is it because it seems so **dirty**?

You're supposed to phone her Tuesday night after 9:00 pm to speak to her in person for the first time. She wants to bring you off on the phone. You want her to. She wants to meet for uninhibited, no strings sex. And she's only 30 minutes drive away.

Did you do it? Did you cheat on your wife? Have you thrown it all away? You know you're playing with fire, but you find it hard to stop. You've always had a self-destruct button and your finger is pressing it now. You know that, but still you can't take your finger off that fucking button. You are weak and pathetic. You've a good life and are loved and cared for. Did you really throw it all away for a fuck or did you see sense and walk away from that hell?

Why do you find it so bloody hard to commit? To anything or anyone? The only thing you've ever committed to is your dogs. Why can't you be faithful? You've cheated on everybody you've ever had.

Really you need to grow up. When you get this, please look back at the monitor as a better person, one who actually understands what love and commitment is and has committed to being committed. (Enough—all this commitment already!)

But you being you—it wouldn't surprise me if the same old arsehole is reading this. Probably alone, very lonely, full of regret, depressed and contemplating suicide again. Why the fuck would want that over what you have now?

You're a fucking complex, very strange, person. You can't fathom yourself out at all. A complete fuck-up.

WRITTEN: April 11, 2004
SENT: May 11, 2004

Dear FutureMe,

Well, you've made it a full year hopefully without a drink. Imagine what your life would have been like by now if you hadn't quit. I'd say go out and have a drink on me, but why don't you just kiss your wife and be thankful for what you have.

Love you bud,
M.

WRITTEN: July 27, 2006
SENT: June 04, 2007

403 days

Right now at this very moment all you can think about is your past and how you really haven't done much to improve yourself… you're contemplating whether you want to continue down the already beaten path from two years ago… you are in love with the high… even though everything about it is fake and will never stay like that forever… all this fun you're having right now will eventually fade and it'll just be a struggle again just to survive yourself… this is so sad… you know exactly how this is going to end and yet that still doesn't stop you from unavoidably destroying yourself… all you want right now at this point in your life is to be loved pretty much by everyone… rejection fucking destroys you… it doesn't matter who it is or why if someone doesn't want you or like you or whatever… you turn into this freak that is just out to please everyone… and then you look around and wonder why you feel so used up…

You're a liar too… come to think of it… i think you've lied to every person that is important to you in your life at least twice this week… and its not some fucking petty white lie bullshit… its full on fuck yourself over lies if you get caught… which of course in the end you will… one way or another… once again you already know all this and you still continue to do it… why? why? why?

> **"I think you've lied to every person that is important to you in your life at least twice this week…"**

FACE IT!! YOU'RE A FUCKING ADDICT… just admit it already… you're weak and you can't just walk away from it… even after being sober for well over a year and seeing all that you saw and lived and felt and experienced so many amazing things and people—you still think being high is better… won't someone just "lie to me Give me something

worth living for Tell me a reason worth fighting for Give me anything
Anything to keep me breathing"

What is it that scares you so much?... do you do this to yourself out
of fear... maybe when this is read in the future you will have some
answers... hopefully you will still be alive... remember when you
never thought you were going to make it to 18... and you used to laugh
at the thought of that... but here you are 19 years old... but still the
same... hoping you'll make it to next year in one piece... you don't even
care anymore about your stupid fucking rape case... you wish you never
even told anyone about it... maybe. no. of course things would be different... but instead they are like this... that stupid fucking guy... you have
no clue what happened to you that night... no one really does... but you
know... you know something very wrong happened that night... and
there is nothing you can do about it at all... just shove it in your closet
with the rest of you ghosts and skeletons and hope it will collect just as
much dust as everything else that you can't see it so you won't remember
it... I don't know what the fuck I want to do with my life... my brain
and aching body just tells me to go get super fucking twacked out and
forget about all this stupid shit... but my heart says... well... its says to
fucking LEAVE again... you don't know where... but you know if you
run again it'll be a little better... but you're still running... awww fuck
it... and fuck this stupid letter... who do you think you are fooling???
NO ONE!!! you are never going to change... no matter how hard you
try... this—this thing—this problem—whatever it is—addiction (ugh... I
hate that word... only because its the truth) and the truth always fucking
hurts... this shit will always follow you wherever you go... I can't run
forever... but that's all I know... I'm tired

WRITTEN: July 29, 2004
SENT: August 29, 2004

204

Dear FutureMe,

You quit smoking yesterday, well, mostly. You did smoke those stale cigarettes you had in the car. And then there was the one you had to tape back together. But today you haven't had one and I'm wondering if you still haven't had one. I hope not. Smoking really sucks and J. is so proud of you and happy that you're quitting.

You should never have started. You should have listened to all those adults who told you, when you were a teenager, to never start smoking. You should have remembered your dad and how much you hated his cigarettes. I'd like to tell every young person I meet to never, ever smoke. The addiction sucks you in and it's very slippery.

But I'm past all that today and in 6 months, when you get this email, I hope you're even further past it.

Love,
Me

WRITTEN: July 08, 2005
SENT: January 08, 2007

> **"You did smoke those stale cigarettes you had in the car. And then there was the one you had to tape back together. But today you haven't had one ..."**

Dear FutureMe,

Ha! you were wrong ... the world didn't self distruct!

WRITTEN: December 11, 2004
SENDING: December 25, 2012

Dear FutureMe,

Remember MySpace? well I still have one.

Remember your drinking experience? well it happened about two months ago and c., m., and e. m. got you drunk. That was a night I promised i would never forget. so here it is:

This was right after t.'s party (which we couldn't get into), then B. said he would have a party at his aunts house while she was away (which didn't happen cuz B. pussed out).

So we wanna get drunk right, so B. calls c., m., and w. come by the park where B. and I parked our cars, then I follow them to safeway where they are going to steal alchohol, but then m. calls e., who just returned from college for the summer, and e. and his friend decide to get us alcohol. So we go back to M.'s house, E. shows up, we tell him to get smironoff and beer so he returns with a handle of smironoff and coors and we pay him $25. B. and I drink some smironoff with cola, then like two shots of pure vodka, then finish it off with two beers. (b. didn't drink as much as I did) Then b. and I, which had planned this out from the beginning (the original plan was to tell each of our parents we were sleeping at each others houses, then we would crash at b.'s aunts house, but she lived in saratoga and c. and w. and m. didn't want to drive us all the way there), so instead w. drove me and b. back to where we parked originally (at the park) and we decided we would just sleep in our cars. (at this point it's about 12 o'clock.) W. gets picked up by m. and c. and they go off. Then a group of teenage hooligans wonders over to us (I want to get in our cars but B. say to stand our ground, so we do), and they want us to drive them to safeway so they can buy alchohol, but I'm way to drunk for that, so we tell them we can't they plead but we say no over and over till they say "fine we will give you 30 min. to sober up then we will come back and you can take us", but we don't believe they will come back so we try t go to sleep in our cars, then they return 30 min. later. They start shaking our cars and running on top of them and shit, so b. calls me and says we should drive a bit away from them so we do. I am really angry cuz what they did so I back up really fast and intentionally hit this girl. she lands on the back of my car and I screech away. they throw shit at our cars and we drive up to a street right before c.'s street. There b. tells me that his window was broken by those bastards so we call M. m., he won't help. B. decides that he will drive to my house park his car and run back. while he is gone I call E., E. comes and picks me up, and B. drives my car back to my house. E. drops me off, and we fall asleep at my house and pretend in the morning that b.'s car got broken into. Our parents are angry because my mom called b.'s mom and told them they were at our house. so they found out how we told them that we were sleeping at each others houses. we tell them that we were stupid, didn't think it through and we went to starbucks in los gatos last night. They believe us.

that was our first night drunk.

WRITTEN: August 19, 2005
SENT: June 05, 2007

Dear FutureMe,

So. I'm leaving DC. So far I've managed to do pretty much everything other than what I needed to do (didn't pay off credit cards, defer loans, pack things, sell things, get rid of things, etc.).

I've managed to end one relationship in a fiery plane crash. It was only TWO MONTHS, how could that possibly elicit two different three hour crying sessions?

All the while I started, maintained and fostered an empty relationship that looks the way it should but definitely doesn't feel that way. It doesn't feel like much of anything other than annoyance and vanity.

Then I had sex with my ex-girlfriend out of the blue SIX MONTHS after I'd ended the relationship. It was the best sex you'd had in your entire life. What the hell does that mean? You dropped the L-bomb and you MEANT it, now you're leaving forever? Why fuck with her mind like that? Why fuck with your own mind like that? There are times when you love somebody and it's better for them not to know it. It was more than goodbye sex, it was "in another time and place we would've been together forever" sex. And now you have to live with that. This wasn't driven by a desire for sex, it was driven by a mutual desire to be close to one another, to feel that energy again. Sometimes love is like crack, you want it more than anything in the world and convince yourself that those brief glimpses at what a relationship can be are worth all of the other shit that comes along with it.

> "It's like I start fires with people and never bother to put them out."

Now I'm frantically scrambling to tie up all of my loose ends. I'm taking a trip to California right in the middle of it all because I love to indulge myself like that. Do I have the money for it? No. Do I have the time? No. Do I really give a shit? Not really.

Then I come back and am faced with saying my goodbyes to all of the good friends I've made here. It's like I start fires with people and never bother to put them out. I have intense conversations, delve deeper into personal and emotional topics than most others do, and as a result I form

208

real and lasting bonds with what were formerly complete strangers. The problem is that I do this with SO MANY PEOPLE. I am never content to have a group of close friends and have that be enough. I have my friends here, my friends there, my ex-girlfriends that I never fully sever contact with, and everyone else that I've shared a bond with. Sometimes BONDS BREAK, simply because there isn't enough time in the day or real atten-tion to be paid to make them worth keeping. The problem is that they're ALL worth keeping. How am I to decide who stays and who goes?

There are a lot of shitty people in the world. There are also a lot of amazing people. I find an amazing person and I don't want to let them go. I want to sur-round myself with them, I want to be tied to them somehow so that I might continue to feed off of their energy and understand what their perspective on the world is so that I can enrich my own. I want to see where our paths take us and where they might cross so that I can have another intense conversation, another fruitful discussion. I want to learn and grow and see how other interesting people are doing the same.

> **"I want to be tied to them somehow so that I might continue to feed off their energy and understand what their perspective on the world is ..."**

Then I go home to South Dakota. I see my high school friends. I've changed. A lot. Some of them haven't. Will they think that because I've changed we can no longer be friends? What parts of me have changed? What insights into myself will my old friends give me? It's hard for me to do the "let's have a few drinks and remember old times" chats. I want to have

209

a real conversation with the person you are NOW, and I want you to do the same with me. It's worth it. It's emotionally and intellectually draining.

Then I ship off into the heart of darkness. Zambia. I have no idea what to expect. I think I've changed so much upon my entrance into the urban life, the working life, the east coast. What about a move to a culture so entirely different from your own that it's hardly recognizable as an American as a "real" life? I'll be working with the land, working with people, helping. Helping myself understand the way people used to live and how we hopefully still can: SUSTAINABLY. They may be starving for food in Zambia, but we're starving for meaning and FEELING here in the U.S. I will gain so many insights and experiences while I'm there, and I will surely continue to change. Markedly. Then I come home again and do it all over again.

At what point does my life in South Dakota become meaningless except as a distant memory? When do my high school friendships become relics of a time passed? I want them to be living, to be real. I want them to grow with me and remind me that I was who I was but that doesn't mean that I've changed so completely that it isn't a part of who I am today. I always want it to be a living part of me.

I strive for continuity. I strive for community. I strive for meaning. But in so doing I preserve and create connections between so many disparate events and people in my life that it becomes difficult to derive any of the three aforementioned qualities from any of it. It's simply a convoluted mess, devoid of any underlying pattern or structure. My life is my canvas. I've painted nearly a third of it (a quarter if I'm optimistic here at 23) and it's already so schizophrenically colorful, intricate, and dizzyingly amorphous that I can't imagine that it will come together as a single work of art that can be appreciated any more than those stupid fucking splatter paintings are.

The answer: there is none. I can only continue to be me and do the best I can to make sure that I'm true to myself and continue to do those things that I believe will help me best realize and optimize my abilities so that I might effect positive change in some way. My life wasn't mean to be static, it wasn't meant to be easy. I truly believe that I was meant to be a semi-transient being, torturing myself with the emptiness that I feel while settling for nothing less. The comfort that I seek is an illusion, I would never be satisfied with a sedentary life. I am doomed to continue moving and seeking and building and growing and dying and destroying and stopping until I've tramped the globe and satisfied myself that there is no Truth, there is no Love, and there is no such fucking thing as Contentment. To be content is to stop searching for something greater, and until I either find or create that I will not rest.

"I truly believe that I was meant to be a semi-transient being, torturing myself with the emptiness that I feel while settling for nothing less."

How fucking pretentious is that? What makes me think that I'm too good for an office job, that I'm too good to settle down? Why can't I just COMMIT to something and build my meaning and my truth around that? It's possible to find everything I'm looking for in a village without ever leaving. It's possible to find that by devoting yourself to a trade or study. Maybe it's a fear that if I do finally devote myself to one place or one hobby or one job that I will devote years and years of my life to it before failing. I would rather have tried everything and say, "Look, I failed, but damn did I have a lot of adventures on the way." I hate the idea of looking back on my life and thinking, "I was happy enough, but somewhere deep inside I just KNOW that the part of me that still remains empty today could have been filled had I looked a little harder."

Maybe we all die with that empty feeling. We all build our lives. They are our fortresses. They are the things we point to and say, "See here? This is my LIFE. Isn't it wonderful? Look at all the great people I've met, the passion I've felt, the things I've accomplished. That's my life and I'm so fucking happy that it's mine." I want the Sistine Chapel, not a ranch-style home in the suburbs. The question is, am I capable of building it or am I dooming myself to failure by not being satisfied with what I am capable of?

One thing's for sure, I'm capable of rambling on and on and on and on and on and on and on.

WRITTEN: August 01, 2005
SENT: November 19, 2007

Dear FutureMe,

i want to tell you that this year you need to obtain control of the city.

WRITTEN: May 31, 2005
SENT: January 01, 2006

215 days

Dear FutureMe,

this year you need to take control of the region.

WRITTEN: May 31, 2005
SENT: January 01, 2007

Dear FutureMe,

this year you must take control of the country.

WRITTEN: May 31, 2005
SENDING: January 01, 2008

Dear FutureMe,

this year you must take the earth in savage but truthful tyranny.

WRITTEN: May 31, 2005
SENDING: January 01, 2009

Dear FutureMe,

you already take the whole earth in control, but you must not stop!
There's a whole universe to obtain … and beyond … Hail M.! Hail! Hail!

WRITTEN: May 31, 2005
SENDING: January 01, 2010

Okay. Firstly, I hope you still have this email address. You need to … keep checking it. As of 2004, you've had it for six months. Hopefully you didn't subcome (sp) to V.'s temptation for multiple email acounts.

I trust this Christmas finds you a little less pesimistic, and a little more accepting of how other peeps celebrate the season. I recall last Christmas you were more than a little frustrated with peeps saying that you had to be joyful. No, you don't have to be joyful. You can't create a feeling; but the point is that hopefully you learned to accomidate other peeps in order to help them appreciate God's gift for this season.

Though, you never did get frustrated with God because he didn't exist. You got frustrated for two reasons A) You sinned, and sinned bad, causing you to fall into despair, or you B) God didn't seem to follow through on a prayer of yours. You never did have a hard time disbelieving in Jesus or the existence of God (You were always too intelectual to do that), but you knew that a person's words are useless unless they square with reality. Hence, your past year was probably spent learning on how to apply Jesus's words on prayer to actual experience. You even bought more than a few books on that subject. I hope you are more enlightened on that prospect.

> **"… you knew that a person's words are useless unless they square with reality."**

I would take this time to find some people to spiritually pour into, if you aren't doing it already. You always did feel better when you were helping someone else with their dreams.

Regarding your afro dreams … I hope you didn't try it again this year, and if you did I hope you have some good reasons! If not, shave it off and buy yourself a hat!

For a kid with no life, you have a lot to say. This is a good habit, and I encourage you to stir this up and use it towards writing.

Blessings, Peace, Truth, ect, ect ect. Have fun for the next year!

WRITTEN: March 27, 2004
SENT: December 15, 2004

Dear FutureMe,

Me and you have just been thinking after browsing the FutureMe website how similar people are ... ambitious, contemplative, comic, and deep down quite aware how wonderful we are. I guess you have to be a little optimistic to write to the future. Though today on your walk to work you decided that the future does not exist in a complex train of thought that left you feeling quite brilliant at the time but that in retrospect is hardly original.

I wish you could remember this sense of comraderie when you are meeting people, or remeeting people, or even talking to the people you live with. I wish you were thinking less about how you looked and more about the wonderful things that may be inside this fellow human. I wish the people in your neighborhood smiled when they walked by and didn't wait until you are two feet apart to make awkward eye contact and perhaps offer a grim smile. I wish

> **"Me and you have just been thinking how similar people are ... ambitious, contemplative, comic, and deep down quite aware how wonderful we are."**

215

you could even remember the names of the people who live in your apartment building. I wish people weren't afraid.

Tonight there was a tremendous thunderstorm while you were at work and a tornado touched down somewhere in your city. You didn't know any of this until you got home and heard phone messages from people calling to ask if you were alright. It was rather strange to have lived through something trying without even knowing it.

I hope you had a wonderful time dancing tomorrow night. I hope you wear something slightly shocking and laugh and drink more than is good for you and forget, for awhile, the analytical contemplative self sitting and thinking inside you for a few frivolous hours. You are twenty-one and deserve to have fun.

I love you
—Me

WRITTEN: June 24, 2004
SENT: August 24, 2004

Dear FutureMe,

Three decades ago, you were sitting around, browsing the web (does that even exist anymore?), checking out FutureMe.org, and writing to yourself. Damn you were boring.

Your birthday is in a week. You're gonna be how old? The 'right now' me is going to be 25 in a week's time. That means you're gonna be 55 years old!

Damn.

What have you done with the last three decades? Did you make a change in the world?

You used to be a political fire-brand. An unabashed liberal. Not afraid to stand up for what you believed in. The big question is, are you still???

Or did you wuss out, buy a house, start a family and get old, fat and lazy? Did you get content? Please tell me you didn't.

If you did, why?

Ahh well … Kids these days, eh? :)

Remember, though. Even if, at age 54 (soon to be 55) you feel like no one loves you,

"You used to be a political fire-brand. An unabashed liberal. Not afraid to stand up for what you believed in. The big question is, are you still???"

you're too old to make a change anymore, etc etc etc, remember something. THAT'S BULLSHIT. You can ALWAYS make a change. You can ALWAYS make things better. And I (you) will always love you. If no one else does, I DO. ALWAYS.

Ahh well … Peace out, man. Keep fighting the good fight. And maybe you'll have a beer for yourself today, eh? If ya made it this far, you deserve it … !!! :)

WRITTEN: September 03, 2004
SENDING: September 03, 2034

Dear FutureMe,

Did you go to space yet or what? Get off your butt and go bounce on the moon—what the hell is keeping you—too expensive? You need some space buddies.

Aliens land yet?—Did you get their help go to Space and fly around Mars. Because you know you needed them damn pesky aliens to come down and whisk you off. NASA have their thumb up their ass and deny any real leaps in technology. They still Bullshitting people??

If you did go—How was it? Dark and Spacey hey. Thats what I thought. Did you take some pictures with some new kind of 3-D Camera? Good job—I will start looking forward to it now.

Later Space Cadet. (Happy Birthday by the way.)

WRITTEN: August 01, 2006
SENDING: August 15, 2023

6223 days

Hey me,

It's you (aka me). Anyways, there's this time traveler's convention on May 7th, 2005 and if time travel is possible, I'd like for you (well, me, so to speak) to attend. Here is the information:

May 7, 2005, 10:00pm EDT
(08 May 2005 02:00:00
UTC)
(event starts at 7:00pm)
East Campus Courtyard,
MIT
42:21:36.025°N,
71:05:16.332°W
(42.360007, -071.087870 in
decimal degrees)

> **"Eventually, if time travel is ever possible, a time traveler will hear about it and go back in time and attend the convention."**

If time travel is indeed possible in 2035, attend this convention. If not, tell your friends (if you even have any), children (if you have any), or at least a stranger on the street and give them the coordinates on ACID FREE PAPER. Tell them to keep it and pass it down to their children and their children's children, etc. Eventually, if time travel is ever possible, a time traveler will hear about it and go back in time and attend the convention. It'll be great, I might be there—at least, the current me. It'd be great if you showed up. So go, man.

-PastYou

WRITTEN: May 03, 2005
SENDING: May 06, 2035

Dear FutureMe,

Let the past go.

(You'll be happier that way.)

WRITTEN: March 24, 2006
SENT: March 24, 2007

Dear FutureMe,

Drugs fucking suck. No, srsly. They do. Stop fucking around with them. You feel like shit right now and it's all your own fault. QUIT BEING A PUSSY.

WRITTEN: June 03, 2006
SENT: January 15, 2007

Dear FutureMe,

Wow. You're 30. Is it weird? Do you feel old? You're only 2 years older than you were when you wrote this, so you shouldn't freak out, just in case you are.

If you are in med school, Congrats! I knew we could do it! It was just a matter of overcoming ennui and laziness. Life is much more interesting when you make the effort to dig for knowledge. Like, you can form your own opinions and stuff. No more depending upon the hearsay and conjecture that passes as truth among so many.

Are you still in love with the absolute wrong person? I bet you are. But I bet that you have also moved on to someone else. I hope he is one that more or less fits without too much discomfort.

Remember to not compromise on passion. If you feel indifferent about this guy, don't let it get serious. You don't need to have someone there all the time. You, of all people, know this.

Barring tragic accident or disease, you are probably going to live well into your 100's. Think of that. At least 70 more years of learning and seeing and tasting and laughing and crying and books and TV and movies and travel and sex and love and friends and death and birth and everything that you have never experienced. It is all out there. More than can be experienced in multiple lifetimes. Don't ignore it.

I bet these 28-year-old ramblings sound a touch naive to you, huh? I bet you're all adult and wise and holier-than-thou, especially now that you are in med school.

> **"Remember to not compromise on passion."**

Well, stop it! 30 is nothing. You're still a child. Still too many things out there to discover. Still too many pre-conceived notions that need to be smashed.

WRITTEN: June 11, 2006
SENDING: June 07, 2008

Dear K.,

I'm writing to you, well, me actually. I'm writing here just to remind you of some of the recent events, good and bad.

Last week Aunt N. died. It was a rough experience. Gram walked into her apartment and found her dead in her bed. I couldn't imagine what she was going through and may still be going through now. I was upset because Aunt B. asked me two weeks prior to her death not to take Aunt N. out because her children wouldn't approve. There was a lot of drama with them and not wanting us to "interfere". I felt guilty for not taking her out because that was one of the last conversations I ever had with her. I feel like I should have disregarded Aunt B.'s warnings and done what was right, treated my Aunt N. as someone I loved and cared for.

When I saw Aunt N. in the casket, it was difficult. She didn't look like herself. She looked more like herself when I saw her in her bed that day she died. In the casket though, her hair was brushed back rather than curled. They had plucked her moustache hairs and eyebrows. She didn't have any lipstick on. She wasn't my Aunt N. then. I couldn't stop looking at her and in turn could not stop crying.

Today I took J. to a local festival at St. Thomas More. He had been talking all year round about when the festivals were coming to town. Instead of riding all the rides he would normally ride, he freaked out and only went on four of them.

I went down the giant slide with him. I'm scared of heights and get motion sick, so this probably wasn't the best idea, but anything for my boy. We started down the slide and I began screaming, oblivious to the little lump of 4-year-old on my lap. I was grabbing onto the side of the slide, pressing my feet onto the burlap sack just trying to get it to slow down. My dad was with us and took a picture just before we got to the bottom.

I'm screaming and turning sideways on the slide while J. is looking terrified. Being that I was the biggest and heaviest of the three slide riders at the time, I built up a little more momentum and plowed down two children at the base of the slide.

When we got home later, J. and I made snow cones with our new snow cone machine. Then we went outside and I began to teach him a different way to learn to ride his "two-wheeler."

A few weeks ago he asked me to take off his training wheels so he could ride a two-wheeler. I agreed, thought it might be a little too soon, but figured we'd try. It didn't go too well. He was more intent on staring at all the wonderous things around him than paying attention to balance and steering.

"I went down the giant slide with him. I'm scared of heights and get motion sick, so this probably wasn't the best idea ..."

So today, I put one of the training wheels back on. I walked with him as he pedaled. After a few minutes of back and forth on the sidewalk, he picked it up rather quickly. As long as he didn't turn around to talk to me while riding, he stayed upright. Much of the time he rode on the two main wheels only resting on the training wheel occasionally.

I really was so very proud of him. It took a lot of encouragement to get him to keep trying: "You're doing so good! I'm so proud of you! Look at you go! Give me a hug! You're getting so big!" He ate that stuff up. So I'm thinking that maybe a couple more sessions of riding like this and I'll be able to take off that last training wheel and see how we do.

Well, it's time to get to bed now as it's 12:52 and I'm going to Reunion in the morning. I hope you're doing well and getting more sleep now that you did a year ago.

Love,
K.

WRITTEN: June 25, 2006
SENT: June 24, 2007

Dear FutureMe,

It's been four years since university. You don't know where J. may be lurking—she says she will burn the house down if you don't move away from your parents, and J. does good on her promises, so, yeah … maybe it's time to start packing.

WRITTEN: March 24, 2006
SENDING: June 10, 2010

1539 days

Dear FutureMe,

right now, you do not have a real job. you are living on child support
and the good graces of your city work. the boys are out of school for
the summer. and you manage to spend very little time with them, even
though you have nothing better to do.

i hope you've improved things since now. have you met a man yet? i
mean seriously, before you are too old to do "it."

still making house payments on time? that's very important, more important than getting any of the other bills on time.

are you still pudgy? do something about that already!

and seriously, next time you write one of these, be a little more upbeat
about it.

WRITTEN: June 26, 2006
SENT: June 26, 2007

Dear FutureMe,

You may not remember
this time when you sat at
a starbucks and listened to
the people around you, the
music overhead, and the

> **"Hold on to the notion,
> however foolish, that life
> is all around you every
> moment of every day."**

hiss of the steam of the coffee machines. But in this moment, you were
happy. You had grabbed hold of an idea, of an understanding, that life
is not all these "quality" moments which is just an american rationaliza-
tion to allow us to ignore the mundane for its lack of productivity. No,

the mundane productivity of life is critical to it, for giving life texture and richness. Life is a lot of moments of sitting in traffic, of waiting in lines, of sitting in a noisy-as-all-fucking-hell starbucks amidst the din of humanity—and loving life. Hold on to the notion, however foolish, that life is all around you every moment of every day. Not only that, but it's also beautiful, and especially worth living.

WRITTEN: June 27, 2006
SENT: June 29, 2007

Dear FutureMe,

Who would've ever believed how things would turn out? You already knew that life was, in the end, mostly unpredictable. But still, I'm sure you didn't expect to really succeed as well as you have. Your partner is doing better and better as the years pass. Her PTSD and related issues have grown less and less obtrusive for both of you. She is happier than ever. And you two are happier with each other than ever. It still surprises you both that you got married, but, then again, you always said you would do it when everyone had the opportunity to do so. The hateful crowd who tried to ban gay marriage failed after a long fight, and the country you feared was going to become a completely corrupt place caught in a perma-war with everyone, in the end it

> "It still surprises you both that you got married, but, then again, you always said you would do it when everyone had the opportunity to do so."

became a much better place, a beacon of light for other nations, an example worth following. Yeah … It seemed like a fantasy when you wrote this, but sometimes the good overcomes the bad, whatever the hardships in between times.

Your partner is nearing forty years old, now. She is still every bit as lovely a woman as you've ever known. Her smile is a regular feature of your days, and her laughter has somehow become richer, fuller, more life-sustaining than it used to be. The lines in the corners of her eyes are from that laughter, those smiles, the good times you've made together. People are amazed that you two have such an astoundingly good relationship. Personal friends recall how you both struggled through the hard times like they're recounting a myth or a fairy-tale. Maybe it is a bit like that, after all. As you sit together on the porch sipping mojitos, watching cars pass as the heavy drops of a summer rain sound along the tree-lined street, holding hands, you marvel at what dogged persistence can accomplish. You two have that persistence in abundance. You never quit cheering her on, and she—with all that intelligence and passion and desire—found her way up that mountain and stood atop her world. That weariness you sometimes see in her? It's nothing compared to the triumph she's made of her life.

Your boy is eighteen, now. Damn—but how did the time pass? He's strong, healthy, and despite the adolescent need to push buttons and pick at tender spots, he's still as sweet as he was when he was only eight and still completely oblivious. He works hard on himself, and his goals are nearer than ever. He'll graduate college and attain them all, you know.

Your daughter … She's doing so amazingly well! Her mid-twenties are in sight! What a different world she inhabits, now. It's good to have her back in your life, isn't it? You thought that you'd lose her to the distance she grew up in, living so far from you, her naturally reclusive dad, but she fought to pull you out of your shell, appealing to your need of her and your sense of familial ties. Now, she's telling you of her life and giving you her heart, and you are more grateful than you could ever express.

And what of you, my friend, my older self? Have you figured it out, yet? Here you are, nearly fifty years old, with so much to look back on. You've seen your parents die … You never thought you'd take away so much from that experience, as heart-wrenchingly difficult as it was. They brought you into the world and left it before you. Flawed and fallible, they loved you as well as they could, and somehow, in the end, you could forgive them for all the painful errors and oversights. You find that, nowadays, you can forgive all the world. You know that your love demands it of you; your heart doesn't understand grudges, however much it appreciates cynicism. You've learned that you get from the world only what you give it. Has it given you yourself, yet?

"Looking at a paycheck that hardly pays the most important bills, I wonder how I'll ever get out from under the burden of debt."

I wish that you could have written to me, here in 2006. I wish that you could reassure me about what I've written here to you. Truth be told, I'm scared a little bit, because the future is a wildly uncertain place and there are so many, many things I'm hoping will go well for myself and others. Looking at a paycheck that hardly pays the most important bills, I wonder how I'll ever get out from under the burden of debt. Sometimes, I worry that things will go horribly wrong, that the very worst things will come to pass. Sometimes … I fear that I'll be destroyed or, worse, that I will fail those I could never stand to fail.

228

Well, I should probably close this letter. I could write a lot more to you, maybe jog that old man's memory of yours. Did you ever remember that you were going to have this sent to you from back in the day? Haha! And yet, yeah, I kind of do have faith in this technology and the people behind sites like FutureMe.org and my email service provider. Somehow, some way, I expect that this letter will get through to you. My only wishes are that 1) you forgot about this letter and are now happily surprised, and 2) the future has turned out even better than I imagined it in 2006. I really want things to go well, my friend.

I really hope that things went well.

With much love,
I remain…
Myself

PS: The day I wrote this was warm and sunny, 78 degrees

> "Somehow, some way, I expect that this letter will get through to you."

Fahrenheit with a forecast of 98 for the day's high temp., with a possibility of thunderstorms. I was wearing my hemp shoes, Loomstate jeans and an AC/DC "Back in Black" tee I bought at Target for $14. The portable swamp cooler and overhead fan were on. There was food in the house and drinks in the fridge. The day I wrote this, I was pretty much broke, waiting on my paycheck to arrive sometime in the next couple of days, worried about money like field mice worry about birds of prey. The day I wrote this, I missed work because I didn't have enough gas in my champagne colored, four-door 1996 Saturn SL1 to get there and back. The day I wrote this, I was nonetheless happy—happy despite a number of things that might have dragged me down. I was happy because I realized, after writing this letter to you, that I do actually have some real hope in me, in life. The day I wrote this, my life's partner was struggling with a lot of things, but she was already proving that she could, and would, succeed. And my love for her was even greater than the day before.

The day I wrote this, 10 years seemed a long, long way away.

WRITTEN: June 28, 2006
SENDING: June 28, 2016

---

hey future me,

i hope you are more than what i am today. you sent this exactly a year ago. what are you doing now? you've graduated from high school. do you feel more independent? wiser? cooler? hah, you were never cool. i wonder if you managed to weasel your way into harvard.

> "He promised you forever, but 5000 miles can make people forget. I still love him. I hope you don't."

last year you met a great guy, but he's gone now. i wonder if you'll ever meet anyone so kind, smart, and funny. do you remember when he stole a flower from the cafeteria to give to you? do you remember when you guys would sneak out in the middle of the night and walk through the neighborhood? and that one time it rained? he promised you forever, but 5000 miles can make people forget. i still love him. i hope you don't.

get up! get out! live a little before you go on to college. this is your last change to be an immature, irresponsible high school student.

230

i hope i havent made any big mistakes between now and wherever you are when you are reading this.

love yourself, try to see the bright side of things, and i'll see you on the other side.

WRITTEN: June 19, 2006
SENT: June 19, 2007

Dear future J.,

Happy 40th birthday! This is a letter from your past self, sent Wednesday, 5 July 2006, at around noon.

You are living at the house in Denver. You live with and love an angel sent to earth, your beloved beshert, M. The two of you have been together about a year and a half and are stupidly happy, even in the hard times. She is the light of your life and the most beautiful woman in the world.

Loving her is also the best thing that's ever happened to you. You are 100%, flat-out committed to M. You waited your whole life to find someone like her, and now she's here. Remember this, in case you've forgotten: God put you two together, and you're going to be okay.

You aren't Jewish yet. This is frustrating you right now. Your beit din is tentatively scheduled for September, after the interminable Intro to Judaism class ends in August. Your greatest desire that doesn't have to do with M. is to be Jewish. When you convert, you're planning on taking on the mitzvah of tzitzit on a daily basis (wearing a tallit katan) and wearing a kippah every day. You struggle with how that will look if you have full sleeve tattoos, but you're slowly bringing the disparate parts of yourself into reconciliation.

You have a dozen tattoos and are saving up for more. The next one will either be your right arm sleeve (Jewish theme) or left arm sleeve (dragon and phoenix embracing). When you and M. decide about having another baby, you're going to get a chest piece done with the Hebrew names of all the kids, including the baby.

Your children are not yet teenagers. For that matter, you only have four of them. Did that change? You and M. want to have a baby together—your egg, E.'s sperm, and her womb. You're considering the name H., after M.'s grandfather S. Did you ever make her happen? Did Mom and Dad ever accept your baby as their grandchild?

> "Did Mom and Dad ever accept your baby as their grandchild?"

Your parents are your parents. Currently, you're in the middle of writing a letter to them telling them you're converting to Judaism. The real reason you're doing it is for the beit din, because the beit din will probably ask and will probably look askance at you if you haven't told Mom and Dad. Since you are in love with Judaism, you are going to tell them. It's scaring you, but you're determined to make it happen before September. I hope that turned out okay. No matter what, they love you, even if they can't show it.

You love yourself. You hope you still do in the future. You hope you're a fabulous, powerful, together 40-year-old woman. You're overcoming the fucked-up-ness of your fundamentalist past, getting healthier all the time (mostly emotionally, but also physically), and, all things considered, you think you rock hardcore. You've grown exponentially in the last two years and you're damn proud of yourself for it.

You can't *wait* to hit 40 and see how hot you are. For that matter, you can't wait for M. to hit 40 and see how hot she is.

You love your life, you love your girl, and you're so happy to be alive and on this planet, you want to throw your hands in the air and shout. Be happy at 40 and for the rest of your life. I love you.

—J.

WRITTEN: July 05, 2006
SENDING: October 09, 2012

Dear FutureMe,

I just did an excel spreadsheet calculation and I think that if we have continued to invest between my age and your age of 65 we should now have about $1,400,000, assuming 8% returns a year. Hooray for compounding interest! Boo for inflation!

Hopefully you have stuck to this strategy and can now retire and go do something fun. Too bad you're old and crusty and probably need a hip replacement about now.

WRITTEN: January 10, 2006
SENDING: May 10, 2035

Dear FutureMe,

yesterday H. proposed to me... he told me he wants to marry me and believe me this is what i want... i love him and i want to spend all my life with him... i am sending this message to the future, to remind me of this special day, that the love of my life proposed to me during the time we were preparing lunch on Sunday 15th 2006 …

please God, make my dream come true, make us happy and i really hope that when i read this in the future, we will be married and happy …

WRITTEN: January 17, 2006
SENDING: January 15, 2010

Dear FutureMe,

Today is Friday and it sucks. Your wife pretty much hates your guts. Remember? The shower incident? Oh yeah. I wonder what will happen over the next two days. You know and I wish you could tell me. I'll try to do the right thing this weekend. What I do now affects you then …

—PastMe

WRITTEN: February 24, 2006
SENT: February 24, 2007

today is the seventh anniversary of the passing of my beloved grandpa. i hope i went to church today to remember him, and say a prayer for him.

i loved him very much. he was my absolute favorite. when i was little, i used to count down the days til he came from korea to visit us. i loved when he came to visit. he would always bring bags (mom calls them immigration bags) and they were often filled with gifts for me and l. he used to bring us beautiful hanboks, blankets, and other things. i would get really excited when he came. when the time came to take him to lax so he could go back to korea, i would cry for hours.

> "I really loved my grandpa. I wish I could've said goodbye in something more than a card."

i remember when b. was born and grandpa came. i had some jealousy issues because i was so used to all of his attention. but he adored b. with all of his heart and love overflowed from him. i want to love like he did. i still remember this time at costco, we were in line and there was a man in front of us trying to lift a rice bag onto the conveyer belt. my grandpa rushed over to help him. and i remember watching and wondering what he was doing. my dad explained to him that here in america, people dont really do that.

i really loved my grandpa. i wish i could've said goodbye in something more than a card. in that card, i wrote in korean that i hope he got better soon so he could come visit us. but we all knew that wouldnt happen.

my fondest memories are of my grandpa and our walks in the evening. and picking up leaves in our front yard in big black trash bags. and walking to crawford's to buy cheese, so we could make quesadillas. grandpa

235

you did love those quesadillas. and i also remember wanting to be just like him, and he would always eat a lot of oatmeal. so i acquired a taste for it, and i love oatmeal too. he used to make it with a lot of milk and it would be like soup. so thats how i still eat it.

grandpa, you are in heaven now. i can't wait to see you again. i miss you very much.

WRITTEN: June 07, 2006
SENT: May 13, 2007

"I wish someone could say that to me right now. I'm so depressed."

Dear FutureMe,

don't worry one bit. i'll be there right with you. anything you need. i love you always and never forget that cause you're a one of a kind amazing person. i told you i'd still love you no matter what happens and i'll stay true to that. just don't worry cause someday everythings gonna be all right. just trust me like you never have before. i'm not gonna judge you like everybody else might cause that just means they don't know the real you. don't worry cause i'll still be true to my word and love you forever n ever and never ever doubt that.

i wish someone could say that to me right now. I'm so depressed.

WRITTEN: March 14, 2006
SENT: April 14, 2006

Dear FutureMe,

Just so you know I don't intend to become like you are!
I pretend to become even better than you may think you are.
Mark my words. I'll be better than you!

WRITTEN: March 02, 2006
SENDING: December 31, 2036

Dear FutureMe,

When you get this, and consider your life at 27 back when I wrote you this message, you will be inclined to be nostalgic. Don't be. It wasn't all that grand. It was fine, but not much more than that.

Similarly, as I write this, I am inclined to think about you and how great you will be and all the things that you will accomplish. I am mistaken. You will be fine. But, despite your degree from a fancy college and high SAT scores, you will not be President or CEO. You will be somewhat accomplished, with a comfortable income, but feeling like you should be doing more for the good of society. Your mood will ebb and flow, just as mine does now. You will be in decent physical shape, but probably wish you could lose a few pounds—just as I do now.

In truth, FutureMe, we're not all that different, are we?

Sincerely,
PastMe

WRITTEN: July 05, 2006
SENDING: July 05, 2016

> **"In truth, FutureMe, we're not all that different, are we?"**

Index

ABOUT THE AUTHORS

Matt Sly

Jay Patrikios

Matt Sly and Jay Patrikios met in Williamstown, Massachusetts, where both were working for Internet companies. They both ended up in San Francisco a few years later, where they came up with the idea for FutureMe.org. They created the site in their spare time and launched it in 2002. Jay does design. Matt does programming. Jay is currently a designer at Amazon.com, and Matt is a program manager at Microsoft.

Dear FutureMe,

Apparently my future and your past is doing an interview tomorrow on NPR with Scott Simon about FutureMe. You like him—he's funny. And he's a baseball fan.

This is exciting, but I'm feeling a little guilty b/c I have been delinquent with my giving to NPR these past two years. I gave a meager $5 this year. I guess it's mildly defensible given that I am a student.

So, FutureMe, I'm hoping that you are gainfully employed (please?) and that you still listen to NPR frequently, and that you will not only give yourself, but you will make a significant gift in my honor to WNPR in Connecticut.

Thanks,
Past Matt

WRITTEN: March 29, 2007
SENDING: March 29, 2010

Dear FutureMe,

one year ago today, you did an interview about futureme with a radio station out in chico. you followed a commercial for crop fertilizer. lots of farmers heard you and probably didn't understand what you were talking about.

long live futureme!

sincerely,
past jay

WRITTEN: December 21, 2005
SENT: December 21, 2006